For Andrea, Holly and Phoebe, Mom and Dad.

CHAPTERS

1: SA Raises Kiff Kids Able to Cope with a Kak World

2: It's Kiff Now the Sun Has a Job

3: It's Extremely Kiff in South Africa

4: Stop Worrying, the Future Arrived Long Ago

5: Privatisation is Kiff and it Counts

6: Beauty and Climate Collide for a Kiff Life

7: I Think You're Kiff – Will You Be My South African?

8: Our Confusing Balancing Act Makes Mega Kak Impossible

9: Oh Kak, They Moved in Next Door... is That the New 3 Series?

10: South Africa: Semi-Great and Getting Greater

11: Surprise! We're Not Getting Invaded

WELCOME TO A NEW WAY OF THINKING ABOUT SOUTH AFRICA

This book is not a collection of positive things we didn't know about South Africa. It goes further by presenting certain overarching themes of South African life and proving the point that, on the whole, things are getting better. It's easy to get caught up in negative small without appreciating positive big. This book is about the bigger picture many of us miss.

We're too focused on the often demoralising minutiae of South African life. We need to be honest about what's wrong with South Africa, but negativity about South Africa is overdone. It's way overdone. And it's mostly unquestioned.

Take, for example, the often mentioned 'fact' about South Africa being the 'most unequal country in the world'. Utter bollocks. It is based on the Gini coefficient, a very inaccurate way to measure inequality in a society with a huge, incoming-generating informal economy. A vast amount of earning in South Africa takes place within the informal, mostly unrecorded economy. Mr Gini in 1915 never envisioned commerce in Gugs when devising his coefficient.

Read this from Investopedia: "The metric's accuracy is dependent on reliable GDP and income data. Shadow economies and informal economic activity are present in every country. Informal economic activity tends to represent a larger portion of true economic production in developing countries and at the lower end of the income distribution within countries. In both cases, this means that the Gini index of measured incomes will overstate true income inequality." Slam dunk.

The real measure of our income is reflected more accurately in the Stats SA monthly household surveys. Month after month, year after year, increased purchasing of white goods, vehicles, homes and education by South Africans of all classes reveals a nation rising in material wealth as inequality gets a haircut.

Foreigners routinely express surprise about just how amazing South Africa is. I hear this so often from tourists. Surely, then, that tells you something is amiss? Something is indeed amiss: a sense of realism not beset by agendas. To set the record straight about what's really going on, each of the 27 chapters here deals with a different theme. Facts, opinion and humour are used to demonstrate the country is indeed on a general upwards trajectory, from kak to kiff.

There are refreshing, alternate points of view here that most of us have never heard expressed. We all know that crime is a problem, but do we ever celebrate the fact that extremism is not? South Africa is a nation that has always drifted to the centre and that is a fact, as extreme parties from the EFF to the AWB have always sat on the sidelines for lack of widespread voter support.

We worry about the future, but the future has already happened. We fail to grasp that South African parents have worried about the future of their children since before loadshedding, before the Guptas, before Peter Mokaba, before PW Botha, before sanctions, before the armed struggle, before the invasion of Angola, before the National

Party, before Lord Kitchener, before the Frontier Wars, ad infinitum. This strange fear of 'the future' in South Africa can be stretched as far back into the mists of time one needs to go until the point is made to stop worrying. It's far more productive to enjoy each other, the landscape, the climate, the diversity and the strange x factor that delivers a unique quality of life.

There'll be something else to worry about because there's always something else. And yet, if one looks at how the children of those who stayed in South Africa typically turn out; I see active, happy, polite kids. I read about fewer prescriptions and less obesity, but let's not stray.

We were worried about the electricity wheels falling off. In a classic case of perfect timing, South Africa in a climate change world is pulling off a successful leap from coal to renewables. We were pushed, but we jumped, and now we're sailing towards the sweet spot.

We used to think we had a geographic problem – too far from Europe and America, they would say. Today, how things have changed as South Africa finally understands it sits at the crossroads of East and West, with a convenient time zone thrown in for good measure.

We used to think we had an inflation problem until we were exposed to the eye-watering cost of living elsewhere and the fact that it is relatively easy to live very well in South Africa. What's more in these difficult times, a South African under pressure can rapidly and affordably downscale to a simpler way of living virtually overnight.

We are less financially hemmed in by fixed costs we can do nothing about. No serious heating, double-glazing, built-in radiators, piped-in gas nor expensive, weather-related clothing and accessories are commonly required here. A washing line serves for drying appliances and shade cloth amounts to air-conditioning. Most outdoor activities are free. Growing your own is a breeze thanks to the wonderful climate. Live simpler in South Africa.

South Africans of the paler persuasion used to think they were a minority until we realised we have more in common with the rest of South Africa than the rest of Europe, America or Australasia. In South Africa, shared values and common aspirations are uniting us and carrying on the work of Madiba and his compatriots.

It's also comforting to know that South Africa is so far ahead in the reconciliation stakes when virtually all white-majority countries haven't even begun to realise they need to begin dealing with their own murky pasts. And it will come. Imagine leaving South Africa and settling in California to deal with the current question of reparations for slavery.

On the new worry around South Africa's recent diplomatic posturing, there's nothing wrong with making lazy friends work a little harder for your attention. The West has indeed been lazy with our friendship while the Chinese president reserves one of his recent two trips abroad for South Africa. We do not need to choose sides and we should celebrate our continued remarkable international balancing act.

From a continent awash with one-party states, the neighbourhood where we live is more alive with multiparty democracies than ever before. Indeed, ours with several viable options for the average voter, is a much healthier brand of sustainable democracy than the two-party 'duocracy' that masquerades as choice in much of the western world.

When you're too close to the ground, you don't notice the wood for the trees. Place your nose too close to the dashboard and your eyes won't see you're moving forward. When we are too busy noticing potholes we're not appreciating how much easier it is to get around in South Africa today. When we're too busy fussing over the few flying to Perth, we're missing the many driving to Plett. Some old central business districts look terrible. Many new shopping districts look terrific.

Indeed, for those of us who like 'stuff', this country's exploded. We've always enjoyed an innovative retail sector but choice has likewise always been somewhat limited. Remember when you used to ask your cousins coming from overseas for that CD or camera? Today, it's on Takealot.

Post-pandemic South Africa has emerged as a shopper's dream. There is tons of stuff to buy and a variety of ways to get it and pay. Retail's gone mad and so has the country's coffee and food truck culture, amongst others. These last two deserve a chapter of their own. For now, let's just say choice has become a fixture of South African life, from political parties to pastries and coffee beans.

The title of this book, "From Kak to Kiff", can refer to things that used to be kak in South Africa and that have improved. Remember reinstating the death penalty? Whatever your view, it's progress that people hardly mention it anymore because it became distracting. Remember when corruption looked like it was taking hold, only to be swept clean(er)? We got the president we wanted, he's better, let's not have short memories as we celebrate improvement.

We can also think of the move outside the country that we were told was so massive, when it turns out many times more people are sensibly choosing 'semigration'. It's better now that we are retaining more people because they are choosing to be mobile inside the country. They are doing so because our small towns are becoming connected islands of excellence.

On the 'better now from yesterday' front, we can also remember those unhealthy ANC-landslide elections that have been replaced by much slimmer majorities that make politicians work harder. Jacob Zuma and the State Capture years have come and gone, like the AIDS denialism and PAGAD bombings that today seem to have been a feature of a totally different country.

"From Kak to Kiff" can also refer to things that many of us assume are kak but are, upon closer examination, unexpectedly kiff. First and foremost, it's kiff that South Africa has emerged so robust and resilient that no single nasty event will ever have the power to undo the life we continue to enjoy here.

This reminds me of another hallmark of the past I'm glad has gone. There was a time when almost any overseas reporter visiting South Africa shortly after democracy would get himself invited to a meal on the stoep of a typical white South African family.

The head of the household would be very pleasant (in a narrow-minded sort of way) as he calmly outlined how everything's going down the drain, while living in comparative luxury. Then, our reporter would visit the most impoverished township he could find where it would all be a case of 'nothing has changed'.

Finally, things really do seem to have changed as we've moved on from this unfortunate stereotyping. Our society is making strides mixing itself up quite nicely, consigning this sort of lazy trope to the dustbin of media history. From debatably raising hackles before, now it really is unsuited to where we are as a nation.

We need to move on from the vague, irrational fear of something catastrophic happening in South Africa at some undefined future point. Let's stop shrinking into our shoes every time we are shaken by a protest or a politician. The pandemic? We handled that with a degree of South African common sense that was sorely lacking in countries that came up with the most confusing set of nonsense regulations that made daily life a pain.

Our tobacco ban misstep paled into insignificance compared to the Covid-19 hoops developed world citizenry were expected to navigate. And never mind that, did the pandemic not perfectly bring into focus those nutters that are a minority in South Africa but who appear uncomfortably 'next door' in other countries? I'll take my chances here.

Imagine what it must be like to be American in the age of Trump. Now that's embarrassing. Or European in the age of everyone pounding at the door with everything from tanks to boats. Or Australian in the age of actually having to hold a referendum to do the right thing by the indigenous population.

Read on and you'll appreciate that the bigger picture in South Africa has been coming into view for some time now and it's looking better than ever. Schooling in South Africa is a model of choice and a mix of excellence and aspiration with the most important consideration being that more kids are in school than ever before. The fuss over South African diplomacy is overdone because no-one respects a pushover. In any event, SA and the US are friends again. Yawn. Privatisation is spreading like a Californian / Canadian / Australian / Greek wildfire as government enacts legislation and issues invitations to apply in pursuit of a South Africa we're fixing together. There's gender-based progress everywhere as liberal messages take root in a society becoming more tolerant. South Africa is emerging as a progressive country with much in common with liberal societies. Out of millions, 'thousands' are emigrating annually because tens of thousands aren't.

Now, the main reason I wrote this book is because constant negative sentiment, whether it's about a person or a country, is not how you motivate people, employees, or states to fix things. Yes, those who point out what's wrong have a role, but do they have to make a career out of it? Being negative for a living, what a strange direction for one's life to take. Are the parents proud or also a barrel of fun around the braai?

I can think of a handful of well-known and oft-quoted local economists who seem to specialise in predicting South Africa's imminent demise, year after year. They make it sound like we all need to hotfoot it to Auckland, post-haste (presumably economics is a transportable skill – why do they stay?).

And yet, when a certain quarter's over, and the economy grew again, or manufacturing's up and agriculture produces a bumper harvest, no-one takes these purveyors of pessimism to task for more inaccurate predictions. Instead, the next quarter, the journalist calls up the economist once again and asks them for more inaccurate fodder which the emigration consultant gobbles up. You want to talk accountability – what about so-called professionals being held to account for smack talk that damages the country where their children, parents and friends live? I don't get it.

Peeing in your own back yard is a perplexing career choice, as is organising expos to shuttle people out of your country. Or starting podcasts about leaving. It would be unfair of me to pick on people who provide a service to those who can't make it work in South Africa.

However, I can't help wondering, when the emigration crowd drives to work on a beautiful South African day, or when they take their kids to the beach or berg in clothes their wonderful nanny of two decades has diligently prepared; do they think "today I must get more people out"? Do they look at their crisp sav blanc, their deliciously pink venison steak, the view set out before them at no charge, and the incomparably warm and pleasant waiter and think 'this is so kak, I need to get back to the office so fewer people can experience this'?

I don't have a problem with freedom of choice. It's negativity that bothers me because it's country-killing. People are motivated to make things better when they feel inspired and nobody feels inspired when they're constantly being told what's wrong with them.

Where things are indeed kak in South Africa, this book will add another voice to the many who agree the foundations are good here so let's get out there to make the rest better. By highlighting that the trajectory is up, I want to help inspire more of us to flatten out the kinks in that generally upwards trajectory. We need to stop dwelling on the negative for a moment so that we can be inspired to make it all kiff.

Don't get bogged down in the details of now without appreciating the bigger picture. In casual conversation, the same negative opinions are routinely trotted out with little understanding that, on a macro level, things are steadily improving. There are tons of examples in these pages of overarching aspects of South African life that are so much better today or getting there.

Speak to some South Africans and they'll say it's all going to pot and point to alleged hate speech by the usual suspect(s) without understanding that South Africans (currently, 9 out of 10) continue to ignore extremism to continue our love affair with reconciliation and ubuntu.

We're also continuing our love affair where it matters with more integration, diversity and interracial partnerships in South Africa while much of the rest of the world appears more polarised. They say white South Africans are on the decline. Did anyone consider many are, in fact, assimilating and their kids don't look like them?

People will say there's no rule of law here. Rubbish! Read on to discover that South Africa's rules-based society continues to march on and away from the days of driving blitzed with bald tyres; not paying taxes, shirking maintenance responsibilities, paying the domestic peanuts, knocking your spouse about, hiding unregistered weapons in the garage, and so much more you've all forgotten about. Politicians, too, are becoming more accountable with more limitations being placed on what they can do and especially what they can buy and receive.

There is a lot of kak that's changed to kiff in South Africa. There's a lot we all cannot get away with anymore and that's good.

So many of the enormous issues we've faced in the past have melted away, allowing us the luxury of complaining about the same things people everywhere complain about: potholes, creaky infrastructure and crooked politicians.

These pages revel in the obvious truth of South Africa's steady ascendance.

IVAN BOOTH

1

SA Raises Kiff Kids Able to Cope with a Kak World

Hasn't almost every South African watched an online video clip of some two-star calamity unfolding as an American accent in the background completely flips out and we think to ourselves how overdone that is?

There are a few nationalities that have hardened the heck up over the decades and South Africans must be right up there amongst the best able to cope with anything Mother Nature or the madman next door can throw at them.

I read a snippet some time ago about South Africans in Australia and how they were better able to cope with minor trouble when their Aussie neighbours were running around losing it. Crocodile Dundee was motion picture fiction, remember? I wish I could find that excerpt again but I don't really need to because we know Africa isn't for sissies.

Well, she is and she isn't. South Africa is a great place to raise children because they're exposed to so many different things that better prepare them for a difficult world. SA kids of the middling sort receive just the right dose of cushiness coupled with a dash of challenge to come out all right. Ask South African teachers who have had some UK teaching experience if most of those kids are coming out all right.

The average South African child is polite, practical, resilient and happy. I would add that compared to their developed-world counterparts, they're much more likely to be shoes-off outdoorsy, less materialistic and more satisfied.

I've just taken a break (I know, after five paragraphs - let's not overdo it in Africa, remember) and picked my kids up at school. I was delighted to hear: "We didn't have a net daddy, so Lesley was the net." Splashes of Deprivation Lite – good for the soul and good for great kids!

Children everywhere throws tantrums, but visit a South African mall and see how unusual sprawled out and kicking on the floor is here. And then there are the older ones. Ever been afraid to walk past a South African high school? Nope. Ever been afraid your kids are going to get shot up at school? Nope. I've never worried about my kids' safety at school.

Grow up in South Africa and you've received a world-class education in things that matter: how to get along with different races, the importance of a social orientation, developing empathy for the less fortunate who are so often close by, and so on.

South African children are also intimately familiar with different languages and cultures and can intuitively navigate unfamiliar situations with ease. Add the ability to innovate and 'make a plan' when something's gone South and I believe you've got everything you need to raise robust, intelligent and interesting kids, right here.

The above is much more important than you think because you can always move somewhere later on that allows you to achieve maybe a better house or a better car, but once those internal nuts and bolts are set, that's it. So you better choose the right spot for your growing kids and – at least for me and my family – the right spot simply can't be an over the top materialistic society or one that exposes my kids to values that are totally at odds with our own.

There's no need to go into detail regarding the latter values point. Most South African parents who have ever been overseas and witnessed certain behaviour first-hand will know exactly what I mean. Yes, things are changing, the world's producing some kak kids spurred on by parents who themselves were never exposed to the proper ground rules, but for the foreseeable future, our South African kids are alright.

Setting those kiddie nuts and bolts with African sun and soil really does children a tremendous favour and provides them with a unique edge later on in life, wherever they, or their own children, may choose to settle.

Granted, there's a lot of opinion above, so let's now conclude with a quotable factoid from USAid: "The Government of South Africa considers education the highest domestic priority and it receives the greatest share of government spending."

Considering the state of the world, a country that spends most of its income on educating the next generation has most definitely put its priorities in order.

2

It's Kiff Now the Sun Has a Job

I've spoken and written many times in the past about my confidence in South Africa being grounded in the fact that our fundamentals are very solid.

Compare this to the fundamentals in some of the popular emigration destinations for South Africans. You can tell me all you want about the single-digit unemployment rate and the free education assumed to be the norm elsewhere by those who should be better informed. The facts paint a picture of countries less rosey and more thorny.

The ingrained gun culture in one, the hostility of regional neighbours in another, the environmental unsustainability of another, and the national preoccupation with alcohol in many others, to provide just a few examples, all point to precarious futures on the kind of macro scale you should be thinking about if you're trotting out the "kids' future in South Africa" line.

I've written here about South Africa's spending on education being the biggest line item in the national budget, while spending on big boys toys like warships and tanks declines, and now I'd like to point you to another little known foundation fact about SA – South Africans are amongst the world's hardest workers.

Far from sitting under a tree drinking the whole day, a research unit at Oxford University found a few years ago that South African workers actually put in more hours than workers in China and South Korea. And it's up significantly from the early 2000s when we didn't even feature. Now, again; we spend the most on education, we work the hardest and just like it takes time for anything to gather speed, we're getting there because we're (mostly) doing the right things.

And now the sun has a job! South Africa for years had the world's cheapest electricity and yet the gross value of all the goods and services produced in the country has tripled since the mid-1990s. The country made a major blunder by not raising power prices as the economy expanded so new energy infrastructure could be built.

That cock-up is in the past and, as usual, South Africans have risen to the occasion to fix the own goal that is loadshedding. I do like living in a country where the ordinary citizen is empowered, for whatever reason, to take their own future in their hands and shape it.

From about 10 percent of power being produced by renewables just a few years ago, South Africa is in the midst of pulling off a major leapfrog when it comes to green, sustainable power produced by the sun, in particular.

It's pleasantly ironic that the old advertising jingle "Braaivleis, sunny skies and Chevrolet", which was so often trotted out to illustrate the good life in South Africa, is again relevant as we're reminded that the sun remains one of the most important benefits of living in SA. Before, 'sunny skies' hinted at the good life. Today, the sun is ushering in a new, sustainable age in South Africa.

We've done leapfrogs before. In the early 1990s, we went from a country with a paltry 5 000 car phones and a few hundred thousand landlines, to the world's biggest cellular success story. Thanks to the decision to launch the Global System for Mobile Communications (GSM) digital cellular standard at a time when North America was a patchwork of outdated analogue mobile phone systems, we went from zero to hero in the cellular stakes, practically overnight.

We're pulling out that frog again as the output of South Africa's installed solar soars on the back of exponential growth in the value of imported and, now, locally-produced solar panels.

It's getting really interesting here as we show the world how a mix of sources can be used to power a country and, ultimately, increase national resilience in an uncertain world. When it comes to resilience of the grid, here's a quick spot of recent reassurance from BusinessTech: "Investors have calmed down on the grid collapse angle. Analysts, like Intellidex director Peter Attard Montalto, have explained on several occasions that grid collapse is highly unlikely."

What's unfolding in the South African energy arena is the assurance that's we'll never be held to ransom the way energy-dependent Europe was following the invasion of Ukraine. South Africa is moving into the best possible energy position: multiple energy-generating and energy-storing hubs are emerging across the country as consumers and business move to a mix of energy sources. The result is that no one energy-impacting event will be able to stuff us up in the near future.

From a kak slow start, our government has moved rapidly to introduce a mix of public-private partnership solutions in energy. The will is there, the regulations and legislation are signed. The bids are in, the building has begun and, in fact, much new capacity is already online. This move away from the risky situation where one parastatal controls everything in energy is firstly serving as a blueprint for other sectors, and secondly, this is all yet another example of South Africa, as a country, moving in a very positive direction.

The benefits of this transition are already being felt by hundreds of thousands of South African households who first got out the camping gear and then soon bit the bullet and got a proper gas stove professionally installed. Many of us have also noted that since we switched to those nifty battery-powered ceiling bulbs that automatically stay on when the power goes down, an unforeseen benefit has been that we're never in the dark when the power is on but the prepaid runs out. How often we fumbled around in the dark when the prepaid meter caught us unawares! As we can see, Eskom-proofed means ready for anything. And who knows what the human future holds?

South Africans have already watched Sky News in disbelief as the cost of cooking, heating, drying and more rocketed in the Northern Hemisphere and elsewhere while that gas switchover mentioned above has seen our own energy bills plummet. I personally love the fact my own household was forced to switch to gas, finally sort out the geyser blanket, replace the bulbs with the battery backed-up ones and boost the fibre with an affordable mini UPS solution so easily delivered by Takealot. Sorted, cost-effectively.

Many households, businesses - and indeed, communities - have gone further. Yes, it's been painful, and sometimes expensive, but the end result, wow, I'll bet a ton of green frogs, it's been worth it. There are growing legions of perfectly happy South Africans enjoying their resilient home energy islands that provide a tremendous feeling of self-sufficient satisfaction. Who can deny that? After all, haven't traditionally independent-minded South Africans been watching 'American Preppers', transfixed for years as we dreamt about the prepped and off-the-grid lifestyle? Well, now we have it.

When it comes to living slightly more free, one should remember the humble prepaid electricity meter which really has been a kiff and mostly unsung development on the electricity front.

At some 10m meters now installed, the rollout of these budget-friendly devices has been an unqualified success that - like prepaid cellular - is now being emulated in the developed world. And they are continuing to make their way into more South African homes and businesses at the rate of 1m annually, providing a welcome way to not receive a hefty municipal bill at the end of the month.

Prepaid electricity bought almost without noticing during the month further helps South African homeowners who are already receiving relatively low month-end bills from their local authorities. It's kiff only paying for three council line items at the end of the month: refuse, water and rates. What's on your bill, Bill?

When it comes to the many South Africans living in the country's informal settlements, the transition away from

Eskom has brought unexpected benefits. Anecdotal evidence suggests many more poor South Africans have also switched to gas. From cooking and lighting with exceptionally dangerous paraffin, visit any informal settlement today and you'll see gas bottles everywhere.

Gas for cooking, heating and lighting is safe, healthy and much more affordable. Fires still break out in informal settlements. However, I'd guess that many South African lives have been saved because Eskom's diminishing importance re-introduced the middle class to gas and this fuel's safety and affordability has been noticed and adopted by the working class.

Eskom saving lives? That's more than kiff.

3

It's Extremely Kiff in South Africa

It was kak when Julius Malema put on those red overalls and everyone thought the ghost of Che Guevara had left the unfortunate mess that is Cuba and invaded the Woodworker-in-Chief with revolutionary talent.

Then it was kiff when election after election revealed that nought-point-something of one person out of every ten in South Africa wanted to wear overalls permanently. South Africans are aspirational, no-one wants to be the worker forever.

The average South African wants a better life for themselves and their family, and sees work and democracy as the way to achieve a car, a house and an education. The lion's share of us are moderates and far from extremists.

Even the CIC himself has mellowed, Peter Mokaba-style. Remember that so-called firebrand who turned out to be a firefly? Speaking in 2023 on the BBC's HARDTalk programme, Malema noted: "Today I am a 42-year-old married man with children, who has taken responsibility and built a solid party." The school run gets everyone.

If you want extreme, you only need check out Sky and CNN for a dose of truly frightening loons overseas. Yes, we have a few, but we don't have many, and that's the difference. Yes, we've got crime, but there's a total lack of the extremely dangerous gun, knife and fist-based madness that is seeming to infiltrate developed-world societies.

We're just not extreme enough to shoot up a school. We don't want to die in a 'blaze of glory' at the hands of 15 cops. We're not downing 12 lagers and looking to smash heads. My view is that the different colours of the South African Rainbow, far from inciting each other, actually moderate each other.

Even at the height of apartheid, white South Africans were never much interested in the right wing AWB and its comical offshoots. Most laughed along as right wingers fell off their horses and did judo in the veld.

As the right wing rode off into the sunset, militant organisations on the left were also ground into the dust by sensible voters who preferred the more mainstream policies of the ANC.

Enter Julius of the Red Berets. It's extremely true that the EFF was founded as far back as 2013 and yet it still can't muster a convincing double-digit general election showing. No one can deny when the EFF first burst onto the political scene, it worried a lot of people with its aggressive campaigning.

Today, the EFF is indeed noisy but mostly reduced to serving a positive purpose as another voice in a healthy, multiparty democracy. Grassroots South Africans have realised its polarising policies, in-your-face tactics and lack of respect for common decency is not helpful when South Africa needs more - not less - discipline to succeed.

The EFF's mediocre showing in multiple general elections and its moving to meddling in the daily running of restaurants and schools, while engaging in its annual SONA antics, shows just how desperate the party is to escape its narrow band of influence. It long ago typecast itself.

It speaks volumes about the character of ordinary South Africans when a potentially ruinous political party promising the short term fruits of expropriation without compensation can be so roundly rejected at the polls.

Extremist messaging in South Africa mostly goes down like a lead balloon. The proof is in the positive way we interact with each other on a daily basis. The happy truth is that political parties on the extreme left and extreme right never succeed here because South Africans do not naturally hold extreme views fuelled by hatred of each other.

Historically, extremists have tried in vain to cause kak. They always fail. Chris Hani's assassination immediately comes to mind. What happened there? The country's liberation forces were so responsible that Nelson Mandela reminded us that while it was a white man who killed Chris Hani, it was the eyewitness testimony of a white woman that helped bring him to justice. That's quite something. There are countless examples of South Africans most always doing the responsible thing by cooling things down. This ain't the Capitol.

I don't think you can equate the standard South African service delivery protest with its 43 rocks and 6 burning tyres with the organised, terrifying, Covid, BLM and MAGA-related madness that's been going down practically everywhere but here. The out-of-this-world mass violence directed at the police is just not us.

Moving on. Even if you have some perplexing apologetic beliefs about what went down until 1994, no one can deny that there are millions of haves and have nots, perpetrators and victims living together in one unitary republic without a hint of retribution making an appearance. Come on, where in the world do you find that?

I bet many of us have forgotten the 1992 Referendum on ending apartheid that saw more than two-thirds of white South Africans voting to continue negotiations with the liberation movements. This was a minority at the height of its power with only a few truly appreciating that the writing was on the wall. Point me to another example in history where an advantaged minority agreed to continue the process that would see it losing its privileged position in society. I only mention this as another example of rationale, moderate, middle-of-the-road thinking that permeates society here.

Even in the darkest days, South Africa has never rushed to any type of a sustained orgy of violence because while the country has indeed had its share of leading dimwits, we've been blessed with many more responsible leaders who have always taken to the podium to calm the situation. Even in recent times, it's rare for things to get totally out of hand. The message of the Constitution that the right to life trumps everything is getting through.

It truly is remarkable that the ANC was founded on progressive, non-racial principles in 1912 when the majority of South Africans were subject to so many inhumanities. Didn't other unjust societies immediately turn to arms?

In South Africa the armed struggle only commenced in 1961 and for many years remained limited to acts of sabotage. Again, even in the midst of such oppression, South Africans were reluctant to escalate things. Maybe we talk too much with our conferences, commissions, indabas and so on, but don't we prefer that to the world's many violent, intractable conflicts?

The fact that the vast majority of South Africans are moderates was helped by the multiracial nature of the fight against apartheid.

While some may have mixed feelings towards people like Carl Niehaus and Ronnie Kasrils, they and many other people who looked like them made significant contributions towards the anti-apartheid movement.

Their presence, up there, on the liberation stage, was fantastic because it reinforced the mulitracial, moderate message that remains the overwhelming feature of South African life.

4

Stop Worrying, the Future Arrived Long Ago

Being an older parent means recognising that familiar tune as a younger dad at a children's party talks about being worried about his kid's future.

The writer Alan Paton, as far back as 1957, noted in a television interview that people leaving South Africa were "perhaps worried about the future of their children". 1957!

Most of us clearly don't realise the future in South Africa already happened somewhere between Nelson Mandela getting out of jail and Jacob Zuma going in.

This brings me to my favourite quote by Stephen Mulholland about my frustrating, inspiring homeland: "I take heart in my 65th year that ever since I was five, people have been telling me that this country has five years left, they always say five years and they've always been wrong."

My dad was worried about the future, his dad, your dad, and perhaps Long John Silver from Treasure Island was also worried about the future of South Africa. We can stretch the peculiar and irrational fear of the future in South Africa all the way back to previous centuries. It's the future now and this is how it looks: non-racial, democratic, capitalist. Isn't that what we wanted?

Drill down deeper and you can add more words to describe South Africa: non-aligned, largely-privatised, and steadily growing. When one talks about the future in South Africa, it's dishonest to focus on the minutiae of the barnacles on the hull without acknowledging the ship has been well-built, is of some impressive tonnage and continues to move forward, albeit slowly. Yes, the sails are a bit stuffed but we've got the oars and plenty of us want to take our seats in the sun and help propel the good ship SAS Kiff forward.

Unless things are getting truly catastrophic, it's best to put your head down, work hard and make a go of things where you are. Build your home base where you've landed up. Knuckle down and own your future. All the building blocks of an outstanding quality of life are already here, simply waiting to be assembled and enjoyed by the robust and the creative.

Regardless of where we live, we all worry about the future and we worry more when we have kids. When I went on radio twenty years ago and spoke about reasons to stay in South Africa, I definitely didn't understand how things change when you have kids. You've every right to worry about your kids' future, but good parents everywhere worry about their kids.

If anyone thinks leaving South Africa will immediately make them sleep better at night when their kids slam the front door shut for a night out, you're in for a surprise. Your mind will have turned from thoughts of the remote possibility of a hijacking to the much more likely scenario of interpersonal violence down at the pub and in the street.

While our worries do not include weekly US school shootings, Vancouver drug zombies, houses sliding down hillsides in Auckland, frozen grannies in the UK, rampaging Russian mercenaries chewing on the end bits of Europe, or glistening new Chinese military bases appearing virtually overnight in the sea off Australia, there are indeed things to be concerned about in South Africa.

Fortunately, reality paints the picture of an upper middle income country, more developed and now much better able to cope with adversity compared to the South Africa of 1994 with its GDP a mere third of what it is today.

We've weathered every storm thrown at us, from Day Zero to Covid-19; because this is a complex, diverse, resilient society – this is not your grandfather's Rhodesia with 250 000 well-off people (incidentally, a 1977 episode of 'The Firing Line' revealed that when Ian Smith's government made their Unilateral Declaration of Independence in the late '60s, the majority of the white Rhodesian population had been in the country less than 10 years), everyone else in poverty, and no democratic institutions providing multiple checks and balances.

Africa generally, and South Africa, in particular, is on the up-and-up. Anyone with an understanding of history and how cycles work, will appreciate that the post-colonial reality would inevitably lead to civil wars, one-party states and so on.

The Marxist-Leninist Africa of the 60s, 70s and 80s with its tin-pot dictators is over. The continent is rising and it really would be a tremendously silly thing for anyone to have remained here while PW wagged his finger at the world, to subsequently leave when opportunity thumps its drum.

My prediction for the future of South Africa is more of the same. We'll continue to progress in a zigzag fashion but it will indeed be forward movement - as it has objectively been (sometimes I imagine being able to send an early colonial up in a helicopter and asking them what they think of the scene of development below). There's nothing wrong with slow and steady when it comes to economic growth because it eliminates the boom / bust cycle that creates unsustainable societies and wrecks lives when daddy can't make those payments.

The future of South Africa is assured for those with the humility to get along with anyone, the resilience to find another way and the good humour that connects all those uniquely South African dots.

Vague? Of course! Predictable belongs in another country.

5

Privatisation is Kiff and it Counts

South Africans live in a country where the State finally realised that the necessities of a good life are best provided in partnership.

Better late than never, right? This, in fact, is called progress and it comes when many governments around the world are reversing course on privatisation and interfering where they should not tread.

That South Africa is galloping along to enact legislation to ensure the full participation of the private sector in our mixed economy is now patently obvious and I bet a little surprising to some.

The country's multi-decade drift towards less government interference in the economy has already included privatisation of the iron, steel, petroleum, broadcasting, transport and telecoms industries, amongst many others.

Privatisation, along with a type of mini-federalism that's also now emerging with super mayors and metros, is exactly what many of us wanted.

Liberal wishes have come true in the resurrection of SAA as a privately-owned airline, in Transnet calling for profit-making rail partners, in Eskom opening the floodgates to private power generation, in municipal outsourcing, in privately-managed prisons, fire services and vehicle testing stations, and the list goes on.

What exactly is wrong with this economic model? A two-tier, hybrid approach that plays to different partners' strengths seems a perfectly sensible way to run an economy. Government enables. It has the authority and the tax money while the private sector has the will, the skills and additional financial resources. Together, they / we move South Africa forward, as they / we should. This sounds ideal. Wake up, depart the herd and smell the opportunity!

I don't know many people anywhere in the world who love 'Big Brother' and red tape so much that they would prefer to deal with a government department over a private company, or a combination of the two like we see in the example of the Home Affairs presence in local banks.

When it comes to security, CPFs (Community Policing Forums) have emerged as another brilliant example of South African innovation in public private partnerships (PPP). Hundreds of CPFs enacted in terms of 1995 legislation represent the community and the police within a particular precinct. Residents now feel they have regained a large degree of control over their own neighbourhoods.

There are so many equally-innovative examples of PPP in action that are being developed in South Africa, rolled-out very successfully, and yet, some people still whine about wanting to walk into a 1970s-era post office and mail a letter. No thank you. Who says the system you grew up with has to be the right one, and do I need to provide the obvious example of apartheid?

We need to move away from the thinking that differentiates between the private or public sector provision of services – and dismisses any private sector provision as a government failing. Aren't there private prisons and more overseas?

If a South African citizen is able to efficiently access and experience something, how can it somehow 'not count' because it was delivered by a private firm or through an arranged PPP? The service was delivered in South Africa, by South Africans, to South Africans. It counts!

Incidentally, that there is space in this mixed, growing economy for everyone is demonstrated by the fact that businesses with a turnover of less than R10 million a year are automatically exempt from BEE requirements – I would hesitate to guess this turnover limit covers 90% of small and medium-sized enterprises in South Africa. The perception that anyone in South Africa has to 'give away' shares in their small firm for it to succeed is totally inaccurate.

There are endless opportunities in a country where the State has realised privatisation is the fastest way to deliver kiff. Be irritated by something that doesn't work properly in your community, draft a proposal to help remedy the situation, and often there'll be public and private partners wanting to get involved in your solution.

For people with the foresight to remain in South Africa and get involved in a way that turns ideas into action, meaning and happiness await.

As we sail towards a kiff new, hybrid future powered by the private sector and enabled by the public sector, the final word belongs to the Free Market Foundation of Southern Africa: 'There has been a lot more successful privatisation in South Africa than is generally recognised.'

6

Beauty and Climate Collide For a Kiff Life

It's kak when people downplay the enormous benefit to body and soul of living in a beautiful country. Wasn't the well-known expression 'shoo-wow' first uttered by somebody who flew in at night and woke up in the morning in South Africa?

South Africa's awe-inspiring landscape has clearly been celebrated for thousands of years as humans purposefully made their way South, crossing the Atlantic and the Limpopo to get to the 1.2m square kilometre nature spot we call Mzansi. From possibly a few hundred thousand of us just a few centuries hence, today there are 60 million. South Africa is a magnet for humanity because it is growing and desirable. It's an obvious place to be.

Possibly the first written confirmation of what those fortunate enough to live in South Africa already know came from Sir Francis Drake in 1580. According to this English admiral, the Cape of Good Hope "is a most stately thing and the fairest cape we saw in the whole circumference of the earth". You've probably read that quote a hundred times.

Here's one by Charles Darwin (in an 1836 letter to his sister) that you probably haven't read before: "This is a pretty and singular town; it lies at the foot of an enormous wall (the Table Mountain), which reaches into the clouds, and makes a most imposing barrier. Cape Town is a great inn, on the great highway to the east." Darwin a hundred and some years ago spotted the direction our diplomacy must go.

Capetonians are not the only South Africans living amongst such natural splendour and that's the thing about South Africa. There is an enormous amount of varying types of natural beauty packed into a country of a very convenient size.

Many other countries are beautiful, but live in Perth and one has to cross a continent to see it all. Pretty tricky to do on a long weekend. South Africa's been billed as 'a world in one country'. It's easy enough to experience many different natural ecosystems and cultures in a short space of time. That's the difference. As is the fact that one really can't quite compare a mediocre gum tree to a majestic baobab tree.

You only really appreciate something, as they say, when it's gone. I went to London and was astounded at what counts as a view (I went to Cannes and was astounded at what counts as Camps Bay). The same is true of cityscapes across the world. Tall buildings arranged in the predictable grid-iron pattern and planted on an uninspiring flat landscape are not, in my opinion, worthy of very much praise. And yet, for many cities, that's what they pass off as impressive.

Dubai's the place for work, sure, but don't suggest this unsustainable literal hotspot is somewhere worthy of living long-term. In fact, you can't – when you stop working, they kick you out. That's what you get when you hitch your wagon to a camel. Come to South Africa, we'll show you what's kiff.

Sitting at this very coffee shop table a couple weeks ago, I overheard a group of American tourists saying they had heard South Africa is beautiful. Nothing, however, could have prepared them for how beautiful the place actually is. When South Africans wake up in the morning, what do we do? We arm ourselves with a cup of coffee to steady ourselves before we go outside, lest we pass out all giddy from the sights and sounds. Alright, I'm going a little overboard.

This brings us to the importance of climate. Who can deny the beauty of rural England? Unfortunately, the climate ruins it. The same is true of most of North America and Western Europe. It's breath-taking to walk on a stormy beach in the rain – once in a while. I certainly don't want wet walks to be my only option, day after drizzling day. But that's what happens when you lose your mind and forgo Fourth Beach for fog.

We're not all the same. But honestly, I don't care what job you have for me up North, I'm not going because the weather envelops us and it needs to be kiff. To me, South Africa is the Goldilocks country – the climate is not too hot nor too cold, it's just so flipping right.

After the UK trip mentioned above, I stood on Kloof Road, overlooking Clifton's world-famous beaches, and what lay before me was so over-the-top amazing, that it actually made my heart ache. I will never forget that day and how South Africa took my heart and gave it a little squeeze, just to remind me that's she here. Either that or I forgot to take my beta-blocker that morning.

In an age where many of us are plodding on with jobs simply because we have to, and many more are having to initiate the 'side hustle' to make ends meet, it's vital to at least live somewhere beautiful, if you can. Overseas, this often means living in largely unaffordable, man-made upscale leafy neigbourhoods. Here, Mother Nature makes the beauty and she's pretty good at it.

I'm not saying that every inch of the Rainbow Nation is award-winning, but what's special about South Africa is that the places that are not quite in the running for that tourist guidebook so often do seem to have the best climate. So there you have it, live in South Africa, and you're very likely to either have the best view or the best weather in the world. Often, you'll enjoy both!

While more days of sunshine in a month than most countries experience in a year cannot put a roof over your head, it does mean that roof is less costly. Living under our blue umbrella is decidedly more affordable because there's no question of needing the personal and home accoutrements that necessarily accompany a weather-bound life.

Good weather makes dealing with the challenges of everyday life much more pleasant. The weather in the morning has South Africans asking 'what can I do today?' Overseas, the question becomes 'what can't I do today? (because of this kak rain / snow / fog / rain / snow / fog / repeat)'.

You know you're living in a kak country when just getting to work is a Herculean task dependant on so many variables that seldom seem to perfectly line up. Yes, now and again in SA; taxis will block the N1, the odd tyre will be lit and the heavens will open in the South of Joburg. However, what won't happen is that a whole cluster of events will routinely make your morning commute a total balls-up.

In South Africa; the weather, rolling strike action, supply chain failings, health and safety madness, stupid infrastructure decisions and foolish policy decisions have not been known to come together - as we've seen in Europe - to make it impossible to gather at the water cooler at 8am sharp. The pandemic's over. I want to live somewhere kiff where the climate and the madness don't keep me confined. It's kak when our daily movements are at the mercy of others or the elements.

Let's not pretend that commuting is a breeze for every South African just because it's often sunny. Getting out of bed, however, is indeed a lot easier when there isn't a minus sign behind that Celsius figure.

What's more, the blue skies that often greet us overhead in South Africa make the boss that much easier to deal with. Imagine thinking about those ridiculous 'stretch targets' in the rain. Thinking about them in the sun puts things in perspective. It makes you realise those targets will evaporate at 5pm when it's time for the beach, berg, bush - or beer on that sunny restaurant deck down the road.

7

I Think You're Kiff – Will You Be My South African?

Apartheid was a kak aberration that had to enact the Immorality Act to stop South Africans digging each other.

Of course, South Africans don't just want to get to know each other between the sheets. Isn't it true that when we answer the phone or walk up to a shop counter, doesn't the other Rainbow Person immediately ask 'hello, how are you? Don't you want to live in a country where it's more important to find out how they are than to know who they are? Gosh, I believe I do.

There is a virtual absence of animosity between the different flavours of South African which now co-exist more harmoniously than anyone could have predicted. To live in South Africa today is to be assured of a future in constant contact with a lot of warm people who smile often, express genuine empathy better than most and who are world-class huggers to boot. When South Africans embrace, you know you are being enveloped – it's full body contact with not a pocket of air remaining.

While it's not uniquely South African to want to hold, connect and know more about the other person, no-one can deny this part of the world is awash with the friendliest human beings and that has brushed off on many of the rest of us embedded with that frosty northern hemisphere DNA as we are.

Worried about the future? Surely you want your kids to settle where there are more teeth on display per inch of lips than anywhere else? It's just the best to wake up to blue skies and broad smiles! The outdoor climate that surrounds us has an enormous impact on our quality of life – right? It determines what we'll be able to do that day and so much more.

Equally, the indoor climate created by our fellow human beings determines exactly how we'll be feeling while we're doing things. Will there be a palpable chill in the air that makes us feel glum, or will there be an uplifting, cheery atmosphere emanating from the warm and welcoming nature of South Africans who are naturally so positively inclined towards one another, even after all that water under the bridge? I've seldom set foot in any corporate or government office in South Africa with a smile on my dial and not had it so generously reciprocated.

South Africa is far from polarised and I'm going to suggest a very crude, unsophisticated yet revealing measure that proves we've been fully into each other for some time. The intention of this book is not to provide exact, up-to-the-minute facts and stats that would immediately outdate what's presented here. If you want to split hairs, Google's your go-to.

Now please explain to me, how in the United States and the United Kingdom - which have been presenting themselves as bastions of integration for decades - is it possible that just 3.2% of the US population identifies as mixed race and in the UK, the comparable figure is a lowly 3.0%? It's not even worth mentioning any developed part of Australasia where material, DNA-based integration remains statistically irrelevant.

If developed world societies like the US and UK are so equal, why is there such little commingling where it really counts? In SA, around one in ten of us enjoys a mixed racial ancestry that includes coloured South Africans.

Now, we know mixed race and coloured are not the same in the context of now, but in the context of history, they are. I did say this is a crude measure, but anyone can agree how problematic it is when different races living in the same backyard are simply not interested in getting to know each other in that most basic, human way. To me, it says a lot.

South Africans are interested in getting to know each other and almost every interaction between people of different backgrounds brings with it the usual pleasantries followed by searching questions and a genuine interest in finding out what the other person thinks of that new issue of the day the Minister promises will save us and the Economist predicts will sink us.

We can all identify with what I've just written – these friendly, good-natured, rainbow-tinted conversations happen across the length and breadth of South Africa, every second of every gloriously unpredictable day. Have you ever seen blows exchanged with those opinions? I never have.

The way society here is emerging, it's abundantly clear apartheid was about as un-South African as you can get. We continue to drift closer while the rest of the world just seems to move further apart. You think it's terrible here? You've got it so wrong. We look on - basking in the glow of our candles - with genuine bewilderment as the world swings wildly between incompatible opinions, one more absurdly extreme than the next, as we just, well, mostly get along. There's violence here, but is there hatred? That's an important question – and distinction.

Is it spurious to point out there are more coloured people in South Africa (10m) than mixed race people in America (9m) while adding that the States has six times the population?

Think about it. Perhaps you'll agree the above is another brick in the wall of the argument that says you have a future in South Africa because - at the very least - we're getting closer, lekker close.

South Africans have moved into the same homes, suburbs, schools, offices, shops and parks so easily and so naturally that we really are, for real this time, becoming that Rainbow Nation.

8

Our Confusing Balancing Act Makes Mega Kak Impossible

It was kak when South Africa was a pariah nation, alone in the playground. Today, it's kiff that South Africa walks the non-aligned tightrope with such skill that Pretoria is home to the world's greatest assortment of ambassadors who definitely don't see eye-to-eye.

South Africa continues to pull off one of the most impressive balancing acts in world history – and gets very little credit for it. Have you ever thought of South Africa's foreign policy in these terms? I bet you haven't and why shouldn't we cultivate relations with as many countries as possible out of pure self-interest? The latter is, I'm told, the goal of diplomacy.

If we want to talk diplomacy, and how it's all a big, ridiculous game, think about this: Two months after the United States falsely accused South Africa of supplying Russia with arms to aid its war in Ukraine, the US gave Eskom R24 million. Months later, the US ambassador was still in his post after stating he would 'bet his life' that weapons had been loaded onto a Russian ship in Simon's Town.

By the way, I found a 2022 Russian coin when I was metal detecting opposite a group of penguins not one kilometre from where the Lady R docked. I seriously doubt Russians on a top secret mission would be allowed to disembark and go sightseeing! Once again, US intelligence sucked and dragged us into its murky web. We live in a strange world full of dots the ordinary oke will never connect.

It's kiff that things are developing to the point where the world powers are forced to compete for our affection. China's president made just two trips abroad in 2024 and one of those was to South Africa. Many raise the spectre of 'the future' in SA. Who would've thought during the sanctions era, when hearing a foreign accent was uncommon, that the leader of a billion people would one day be elevating us above 200-plus other countries he could possibly visit.

Who would've thought just last year that the newly-enlarged BRICS bloc would be expanded overnight into a grouping representing 46.5% of the world's population?

South Africa helped found the United Nations Organization, indeed, we wrote its charter! Now, we're a founding and leading member of a new world order.

South Africans used to be panicky about being friends with countries that are not exactly models of freedom. However, I'm getting a sense that it's becoming a case of the ends justify the means. Times are tough, everywhere, and South Africa needs to do what it needs to do. It's kiff that SA is coming of age and suitors are vying for her attention. Why not?

We are remedying the fact that we failed to recognise our pivotal geographic and moral position in the world and for too long made it too easy for too many. How interesting it is that, again, a month after a delegation from the US National Aeronautics and Space Administration (NASA) was in South Africa - NASA is building a communications facility near Matjiesfontein - the Russians opened a space debris detection facility in the North West Province.

The way things are moving along on the diplomatic front, to be welcomed in capitals as diverse as Washington, Kyiv, Moscow, Havana, London, Beijing and Cairo; I'd wager you'd either have to be a citizen of one of the three geographically-Scandinavian countries, or a citizen of a certain African one.

Years ago, many South Africans raised our eyebrows when we heard Cuban engineers and doctors were making their way to our shores. Today, the world's clearly gone (even more) dog-eat-dog and I now say, bring them on. Bring your doctors, captains of state-owned industry and party officials. We've tried the Western diet. It's ok but it's time to add the noodles, and don't forget the rum and cigars.

It's pretty obvious the way the world is going and, bearing this in mind, the South African government has admirably been looking after the interests of every one of us by cultivating diverse relationships while other nations pontificated and destroyed their exports in the process. Faulting South Africa for wanting more, not fewer, bilateral relationships is crazy. Don't you frown as we fail to join your ill-considered, six decade-plus embargo of an impoverished island, buddy.

South Africa does not have the luxury of getting on any high horse. We need to get more fish and we can't do it by fishing in only half the sea. When you speak about the long term future of your children, you must consider how bright it could possibly be when you're setting it up to be focused only on North America, Western Europe and Australasia.

South Africa's geographic position always hinted at something special. From here, it's becoming abundantly clear that Africa is our oyster and the East's a rising beast. Forget the Henley Passport Index, rooted in the old way of thinking as it is – the world's most powerful passport belongs to the country that gets along with everyone.

9

Oh Kak, They Moved in Next Door... is That the New 3 Series?

It's the middle class that makes suburbs shine by trimming those grass verges while keeping the economy ticking over with those flat whites and the milk-of-the-moment.

This is why mom, dad, the 2.1 kids and Peanut have so often been described as 'the bulwark of society'. History and common sense suggest that countries do well when there is a large middle class and no-one is either too rich or too poor.

South Africa does have a lot of poor people but not as many as you think. Your cousins in Canada who left their private school and 2 000 square metres in Joburg for too much snow would want to believe that at least half of us are squatters now. The truth is over 80% of South Africans live in formal housing with far fewer people living in shacks than 20 years ago, according to Stats SA.

There are about 2 200 informal settlements across South Africa's 1.2m square kilometres. That translates into a collection of zinc and pine homes for every 545 square kilometres of the country - not great, but not exactly a squatter camp on every corner, right? As suggested above, the trend is upwards when it comes to formal housing and, for the future, direction is most important, not current numbers.

It definitely isn't wonderful that many people live in temporary structures in South Africa, but the fact that 80% of 60m citizens live in a proper house is indicative of steady progress. I would suggest you take a gander at YouTube to see what's going down in the housing scene in North America.

It's shocking. Forget wood and tin, the home of choice for a growing number of Americans is a thin plastic dome tent and they are on display, kilometre after kilometre, along what used to be America's ritziest streets.

The trend towards living on someone else's couch, on the street, in cars and in tents is on the way up North of Africa and that's very kak for anyone who could soon be meth-addled Meg's de facto neighbour. According to Current Affairs magazine last year: There are enough homeless people in California (160 000) to populate an entire [new] city of their own." Census 2022 reveals there are about 55 000 homeless people in South Africa. Again, not great - but far, far fewer than in just a single American state.

It's kiff that South Africa's middle class has been growing in leaps and bounds since we transitioned away from one of the most unjust societies in the world. Before the mid-1990s, the only black middle class South Africans were a handful of teachers, nurses and civil servants. Just like methodically adding more buoyancy to a boat, South Africa's stability has been steadily increasing for over three decades now as many more black South Africans get fully into tidy verges.

Seriously, while you were moaning about minutiae, millions more South Africans were getting better salaries that enabled them to engage in the consumer-driven purchasing that has always boosted the local economy. For the majority of South Africans, a better life has indeed materialised through material goods and services never consumed before by so many. If microwaves and mirror fridges are the indicators of a better life, things are looking up.

Solid proof of this can be found in the annual General Household Survey produced by Stats SA. Sit me down at the dinner table or stand me around the braai and spout the usual vague negativity and I'll refer you to this very specific piece of well-produced, hard evidence about what's actually going down in South African homes. The truth is every year more of us are able to afford the things that make life easier. South Africans' disposable income is growing.

Sadly, one of the most recent Stats SA household surveys reported that about 11 percent of South African households experience hunger. In the UK, 22% of households reported going hungry, according to the Food Foundation. This is 12% worse than the previous year.

In Australia, two million households are currently experiencing 'severe food insecurity' as they 'have run out of food in the last year due to limited finances', says Australia's Foodbank. There's nothing kiff about anyone going hungry, anywhere, and I think we'll end here.

10

South Africa: Semi-Great and Getting Greater

It's always amazed me that many people who leave South Africa opt to go straight from the (Joburg) northern suburbs directly to the (Sydney) eastern suburbs without so much as a Karoo, Winelands, Midlands or Namaqualand in between. Why deprive your kids of their grandparents and the children's paradise that is Plett, Langebaan, Hermanus, Hogsback, Clarens, Dullstroom or Coffee Bay?

As we have reminded ourselves in this light tome, South Africa is indeed a vast country comprising many more places to live than simply the usual suspects of Joburg, Cape Town, Durban and Gqeberha.

Surely one of the 500 small towns scattered across a country described as 'the most beautiful place on earth' (admittedly, by one Nelson R. Mandela) might be a suitable place in which to remain close to friends, family, culture and investments while experiencing a significant, Rand-denominated quality of life boost?

If you enjoyed the Jacarandas and the best climate in the world but next-door's wall-hopper freaked you out (and it never crossed your mind to try help make things better where you live by joining or donating time or money to the local neighbourhood watch), surely it makes sense to first try a different, local way of life, just down the N1?

It amazes me how an ex-Joburger will rave about his new overseas lifestyle without connecting the dots that it is because he is now enjoying a five-star coastal lifestyle overseas compared to the previous four-star inland one he enjoyed in South Africa. As much as there are benefits to living anywhere, move from the bush to the beach most places in the world and you'll probably end up raving about the latter.

Fortunately, we now have an entire movement (or, at least a brand new word) dedicated to the common sense approach of trying local before going global.

Coined fairly recently, the term 'semigration' describes the trend towards moving to South Africa's smaller towns for quality of life reasons. Of course, 'semigration' has been happening at least since the first Senator built his 'Villa Rustica' somewhere around the bay of Naples when things under Caligula got a little too rough.

Semigration is the word of the moment, but I suspect it's actually more about reaching a certain stage of life than reaching a certain level of gatvol-ness. For clarity, Google 'mid-life crisis'. Whatever the motivation, it really is kiff that semigration has kicked-off as its own thing because now we get to focus on the fact that there are plenty of scaled-down South Africas with mini issues and mega benefits.

Powering this new relocation option is the fact that fibre is now available across the length and breadth of South Africa and where it isn't, high-speed mobile data fills the gap and affordably too, as the cost of wireless continues to plunge. In seven years, South Africa's high-speed fibre Internet subscriptions have skyrocketed from 31 843 to a staggering 1.3m more recently. Our latest census reports brilliant growth in overall web access.

The Citizen, writing post-Covid-19, said: "The last two years have undoubtedly triggered new and exciting internet usage habits across South Africa...". I can already think that some of those habits must involve swimming, kayaking, mountain biking or simply enjoying a walk in any one of the best small towns on earth before that morning Zoom call.

You can bet the poor sods riding any number of unpleasant above or below ground mass transit systems anywhere in the world would dearly want to trade places with the South African remote worker in the satisfied throes of semigration.

When living the semigrant life, South African employees, consultants and small business owners get to affordably experience every day what others have to fork out vast sums for once or twice a year.

You could counter that small town life is accessible to any remote worker, anywhere in the world. Maybe, but the x factor is the hyper competitiveness that's present like a plague in most of the developed world and it makes employees afraid to leave their desks for fear of missing out, or just for fear generally.

While South African corporates continue to embrace guilt-free remote working, much of the world has seen a reversal of the trend. Who hasn't seen pictures of employees overseas sleeping on the office floor? If that was my daughter, I'd give her some advice about moderation and email her boss a remote klap. What a choice: sleep on the floor at work and impress the boss, or enjoy a 6pm tube ride home and piss off the boss because you left too early.

The difference with South African small towns compared to what passes as a pleasant dorp elsewhere, is that they are generally easily reachable along a good highway replete with Wimpys! They usually have a selection of familiar national chains and increasingly excellent fibre or high-speed wireless links. So doing one's chores while doing one's work is very easy.

From a 'nommer asseblief' past where tiny towns shared what used to be called a party line (not the one you're used to), it's phenomenal that an entire connected platteland is now there to be enjoyed by those who want to remain in, or return to, South Africa, but want a slightly less 'interesting' way of life.

South African big city life has a lot going for it now compared to the mind-numbing days of the pre-barista boom. Things were a little safer and a lot swakker when everything closed at 1pm on Saturdays, no-one traded on Sundays and the only evening entertainment that you weren't expected to invent yourself came in the predictable dual flavours of Nu Metro and Ster Kinekor.

Would anyone growing up in the general sleepiness of South African cities just a short while ago ever have thought that suburbs in our big cities would regularly be scooping 'world's coolest places to live' awards?

However, if you think our cities have developed, you should take a drive to towns like the ones listed above. It feels like, since Covid, there are suddenly a lot more places to live a great life in South Africa as so many mid sized towns sparkle in South Africa's crown. And they do sparkle. And they are sustainable and it's all very kiff. Dozens of smaller towns are getting their act together in terms of their connectivity, security and economy. They are on that good national road towards being great places to live.

Visit popular semigration destinations, get talking to the locals and the first thing that becomes abundantly clear is relief at not having to leave South Africa and live like a forever foreigner in someone else's country.

11

Surprise! We're Not Getting Invaded

I used to get hot under my rooinek collar when South Africans believed our major metropolitan areas were also major European cities.

Now, as time has marched on and the African sun has baked the underdone amongst us a little more, it's kiff to interact with those fellow South Africans who look like me and it's clear we've (mostly) all progressed to singing off the same, 11 language song sheet.

Coming of age is a kiff thing. Accept your place in the world and you're one step closer to the happiness that comes from resignation. Did I just write that? Freudian slip, obviously. I mean happiness comes from knowing who, what and where you are in the world. It's the satisfaction of saying, "I'm here and here is a good place to be."

South Africa is in a kiff spot as Europe becomes literally and figuratively hotter but not so hot that we wouldn't want to visit once in a while. It's just a shoot upwards along more or less the same time zone. Gazing upon the imperialist's map that puts Europe in the centre of a flat world, America is to the 'left' and America Lite (see: Kangaroos) is to the 'right'. The rest of a one billion-person continent of opportunity lies immediately North and we've got some of our BRICS buddies (baddies?) fairly close by.

Considering all of this, our position in the world is surely a good one and don't they always tell us to buy a fixer-upper in a good area? Sometimes, I wonder how countries located neither here nor there get noticed. War or disaster is the only time anyone bothers to check out the location of some of these iffy places.

How can anyone planning a holiday or business trip, and gazing at the map, miss the country located at the tip of that continent that sits in the 'middle' of the world? What a fabulous location for marketing purposes! Like South Africa House on Trafalgar Square on a global scale.

With a similar time to Europe, business is easily done and the flying distance is manageable. US airlines now fly direct to South African cities. And there are direct flights to close-by destinations as diverse as Victoria Falls, Zanzibar, Mauritius and the Seychelles. The Cape to Rio yacht race reminds us we have South American neighbours. I mean, who wouldn't want to live in this neck of the woods?

Those of us who bang on about the future of their children (and their grandchildren), and then fly out to Europe and settle in the most historically conflict-ridden of continents, are missing that while South Africa itself has (solvable) issues, Southern Africa continues to get more peaceful generation after generation as Cold War-created kak subsides.

I've always said our issues in South Africa are nothing compared to the mega kak that's going down in the rest of the world. So often, people elsewhere are subject to events totally beyond their control. Here, it seems to me that we at least have the ability to change things for the better. You can fix roads, schools and crime. You can do nothing about those bigger picture issues on Sky News.

You cannot get more blinkered than choosing to live a hop and a skip away from either Russia or China. Sorry, but that's insane. Russia's in (more of) Europe now and China is building naval bases off Australia. A sparrow has no future where eagles hunt. Come on, why do you think both countries are enormous? Is it because they are inward-looking or are they huge because they've always been expansionist? And we know history repeats itself.

I never want to raise future fodder for yet another pointless European or worldwide war that's easy for non-aligned South Africa to stay out of. Trading with the bear and the panda is one thing, that's great – love your Vodka and your plastic goods. Being settled by them, that's quite another. The long term that sees your grandkids and great grandkids being born, that kind of long term looks more secure in Southern Africa.

12

Ambition Rules in South Africa

From a post-colonial mixed bag of amusing one-party states, most African countries are now identified as 'free' by the Washington-based non-profit, Freedom House (that's a lot of hyphens - indeed).

It was terribly kak when the number of democracies in Africa were in the single digits when communism fell in Europe. Today, the reverse is true with the number of authoritarian regimes now in the low digits. With 54 African countries, this borders on the negligible. So our neighbours (above, beyond but not yet the kingdom in-between) are getting their legislative act together and this is excellent news for every African as democracy tends to hinder corruption and boost growth.

In South Africa, the chances of this country ever regressing back to a pre-democracy authoritarian version of its rainbow self are about as remote as Cape independence. When our first democratic elections were held in 1994 and the ANC won by an overwhelming majority that only seemed to increase, many of us thought we went to sleep in multiparty South Africa and woke up in one-party Zimbabwe.

Fortunately, far from democracy ever being under threat in South Africa, it's been kiff to have remained in South Africa to witness first-hand the deepening of democracy as overwhelming majorities are eroded and the law remains firmly on the job.

South Africa's democratic order and institutions are so strong, in fact, that they got rid of Jacob Zuma from political office – permanently. Following an attempted coup, American democracy responded as weakly as the police on the scene. While US democracy is sadly a two-pony show, South African democracy is vibrant, took on those who would corrupt it and has kept going at them with a tenacity that would impress Simon Wiesenthal.

A house is only as good as its foundations, and it bears repeating that the nation state of South Africa is rock-solid because it was laid on the foundations of the best constitution ever written, the builders were Mandela Ltd in partnership with De Klerk (Edms) BPK and at the site braai afterwards, everyone kissed and made up. It's normal for the paint to peel eventually, and for the garden to start looking a bit crazy wild, but Erf South Africa is a gem and can be easily put right. Didn't the solar guys arrive yesterday?

Not every country is fortunate enough to have a collaborative process of renewal under its belt. The UK continues to grapple with the schlep involved in having an unwritten constitution that requires consulting hundreds of court judgments, acts of parliament and more.

So the foundations upon which my children's feet rest are good, and South Africa's continued embrace of reconciliation has been akin to the regular adding of water to strengthen curing concrete. Recently, South Africa's parliament went a step further to boldly strengthen democracy with the passing of the Electoral Amendment Act.

The media says the new law allows for independent candidates to stand as MPs in the National Assembly, but what it really means is that – finally – anyone in South Africa can be President. How kiff is that?

From a political past dominated by the National Party (NP) and African National Congress (ANC), South Africa's politicking got a lot more democratic with the strengthening of the Democratic Alliance (DA) and the entrance of the Economic Freedom Fighters (EFF). So there were two realistic national political choices in South Africa for years and then those national options became three (ANC, DA and EFF) and now - with the passage of the above Act - our choice of the country's president, at least, theoretically skyrockets into the stratosphere as any independent candidate can now stand in provincial and national elections.

After being elected, they could theoretically be voted into the highest office of the land by a majority of National Assembly members. Essentially, the Act has widened the pool of leadership choice for the National Assembly (and provincial legislatures).

It followed the Constitutional Court declaring the country's previous electoral law unconstitutional for only allowing political parties to be represented in provincial and national legislatures. This is milestone, landmark, earth-shattering stuff. And it's gone down with scarcely a nod from the chattering classes. So here's your chance to put down this milestone, landmark, earth-shattering book, and take to Whatsapp to talk the country up for a change. Wouldn't that be kiff?

13

It's Kiff to Connect with Competence

A friend of mine and former South African (can you ever be such a thing?) who swapped the bubble of Joburg's northern suburbs for the bubble of Tel Aviv, visited South Africa recently after a number of years out of the country and could not stop praising the level of customer service he experienced.

The generally-increasing level of competence displayed by the majority of ordinary South Africans in business and government, from cellphone shop employees to bank workers and even the previously sullen types found behind the counter at the local licensing department, is something I have been noticing as much as my friend noticed it on holiday in Plett. I really started noticing it after being called 'luvvie' and 'sweetie' by a home affairs employee who seemed to be multi-limbed as she served three people at once.

Everybody used to complain about customer service in South Africa. Growing up, Cape Town was Slaapstad and the amicable slothfulness of waiters, in particular, was always bleated about every holiday season by the sunburnt upcountry multitudes who could not see the irony in writing letters to the Cape Times complaining about laziness while many had their domestic servants in tow.

The kakness of the private sector's casual approach to getting it right was topped only by every interaction with any government department. And then something started changing and I can even pinpoint when it happened. I was one of the many South Africans in the 1990s who used to dread that annual mission downtown to renew my car licence disc. Such a simple task, it always took a whole morning - back then.

During one of these excruciating forays into the heart of municipal darkness, I was lamenting how I had - once again - forgotten to bring a pen when I noticed an electronic queuing system had been implemented. I remember thinking, 'that's cool, maybe technology will save South Africa'. And it really has.

Somewhere in between battling to set the clock on the VCR thirty years ago and trying to get to grips with SMS twenty years ago, technology seems to have made us all more competent, or at least, enabled our competence.

This seems like a bit of a stretch statement, but there's simply no doubt in my mind that the young South Africans being encountered on the phone, behind Whatsapp chats and across the counter; are incredibly smart, motivated, willing to please, friendly and just awesome. When one thinks of the bigger picture involved here, they put a smile on my dial, warm my heart and make me incredibly hopeful for the future. It's kiff to be able to connect with smart people every day in South Africa who back up brain cells with pearly whites. If you want to be smart and unfriendly, go live in the snow.

Of course there are disappointing exceptions. However, it's much more likely that when one interacts with a South African public or private entity today, expecting to be unable to successfully complete some or other admin-related task, this disappointment-in-the-making now so often turns to pleasant surprise. Don't we then find ourselves Whatsapping the details of our admin-related ecstasy on the trip home? I'm sure you can identify with this. More often than not, we all can.

Who knows why this is happening. Maybe it's South Africa's bigger-than-average annual investment in education or maybe it's the ubiquitous nature of technology today that forces us to really think (at least initially) to figure stuff out. With a mobile penetration rate of over 100% combined with some 80% of South Africans now having access to the mobile web, there's also the fact that opportunities to learn, grow, develop and basically become more literally and figuratively switched-on are instantly on tap.

My take is that South Africans are today more motivated to serve and please each other because we've matured as a diverse nation. When you're one, there's no longer any need to impede anyone's progress. From the days of 'pass one, pass all', we've progressed in the 21st century to a help one, help all society.

14

It's Kiff When it Works and it Mostly Does

Like Switzerland, most things work in South Africa. Unlike Switzerland, our banks don't collapse overnight (under the weight of the looted gold?) and our original flag carrier still flies. If it's possible to go on a tangent before the subject has been introduced, I've done it.

What I meant to write is that it's outrageous slander that South Africans are forced to navigate a web of broken public and private systems, infrastructure and organisations in order to go about their daily lives. Daily life in South Africa is, for the most part, convenient. It's easy to do most things and it's getting easier, thanks to a heavy emphasis on rolling out enabling technologies.

Every time I am told 'everything works' somewhere else, I ask the individual to go into detail and the twin nasties that always come up are – you've guessed it – Eskom and potholes! Another slight tangent: you either get the 'everything works' opinions returning from overseas, or you get the 'it's so much cheaper to live well in South Africa' opinions. And then there are the self-appointed 'realists' in between. Doesn't this again illustrate that life (specifically, the enjoyment of it) runs on opinions and not absolute facts? End of tangent.

Pre-1994, open armed conflict was a real possibility. Today, two of the leading things that really irk South Africans are potholes and Eskom. Of course, while a huge hole in the road and the occasional absence of power are not exactly things to celebrate, it's about perspective. It's also becoming clear that short term electric pain is morphing into something powerfully exciting, as 'solarhoods' emerge to feed their excess electricity back into the grid. The explosion in solar is the most visible positive element associated with our electricity fiasco but there are many others.

For me, the neighbours spilling into the street and into the park when the lights go out is amazing. Forget having to negotiate 'TV turnoff time' – Mama Eskom just flips the switch and the kids happily comply on their way to playing outside. There can be no argument. South African kids, and their parents, are remembering those barefoot days and outside ways.

We're learning to be careful with how we use electricity and we're investigating other ways of powering our lives. In South Africa, many monthly household electricity bills are on the decline, providing much-needed relief, while the rest of the world grapples with rising energy costs.

Back to solar. According to South Africa's electricity regulator, in the first three months of 2023 alone, 2 400MW in new solar and wind projects were registered in this country. To give you a sense of scale: in 2020, 53 MW was registered. In 2021, 135 MW and in 2022, 1 646 MW. That is one of the most clear-cut cases ever of zero to hero, surely. So electricity doesn't yet work here, like it used to, but it will again and it will work renewably which is infinitely better.

Then, on the potholes, give me a break. I mean, if that's the worst you can do... South Africa has the world's tenth largest road network so potholes are bound to make their presence felt.

The problem of potholes is a global one with Britain's potholes being called an 'international embarrassment', according to the UK's Daily Mail. Drivers there have to regularly deal with about 1.5m rim reapers. In New York, every driver is - on average - spending about $3 000 extra on vehicle operating costs thanks to the State's out-of-control pothole problem, says one non-profit. New York State and the UK are, by the way, small, high-density land areas so potholes on their tiny road networks are unforgivable. Let the South Africans know when your road network reaches 754 600 km.

South Africa is like a pristine, white sand beach. You hop off the steps to the beach onto that lovely powdery sand and you amble along towards the water to stub your toe on Eskom and collapse into a pothole. There isn't a place on earth where life is all fun and sun. At least here you get to experience the soft sand in between the sharp bits.

In South Africa, life is 80% kiff and 20% kak (admittedly, not for everyone). Things do work, thanks to the ever-present willingness and ability of business and government to roll-out enabling technology nationally and often almost overnight.

Think then and now when it comes to these essential chores that were always such a low-tech pain in South Africa: renewing your car licence, paying taxes, paying traffic fines, paying a restaurant bill and adding a tip, couriering anything, applying for any government-issued documents, opening a bank account, transferring money to someone, booking a flight, arranging a taxi, ordering in and the list goes on. All of these things now work just as well in South Africa and perhaps better than any first world country.

These are just a few examples for illustrative purposes. So tell me, what doesn't work in South Africa – what are you having such a problem with on a daily basis that you think emigration is your only solution?

Home Affairs, SARS, SAPS and other former red tape fans all now make significant use of simpler forms, text messages, WhatsApp business accounts, online searchable databases and further digital forms of easy interaction that add certainty where before there was only doubt and confusion.

Customers aren't yet treated like royalty in South Africa; but at least the realisation is finally there that they shouldn't be treated like peasants either. South Africa is (getting) simpler, better, faster.

15

Happily Behind the Times in a Kiff South African School

Besides the choice of a puppy or a kitten, what could be more important in a child's life than the school they ultimately attend?

In terms of Section 29 of the Constitution of South Africa, any person is allowed to establish an independent educational institution. Even better, state subsidies to independent schools are permitted.

It therefore appears that South Africa's government has adopted a progressive and enabling approach to education that says if you don't like our schools, you're welcome to start your own and we might even pay towards the running costs.

This is not a case of government failing to provide 100 quality schools, this is a case of government creating the overarching framework that enables the creation of 1 000 quality schools.

Obviously, no-one is suggesting that in the case of a parent finding no suitable school in their area, it's a simple matter of building one's own. I am highlighting the situation on the kind of macro level that few people consider when making those sweeping statements about education in South Africa.

Yes, there are dodgy schools here, there and everywhere in the world; but at least our system is drifting in the right direction of community choice.

This pro-choice, inclusive and accommodating vision for schooling in South Africa must surely serve to reassure those who say they are concerned about the future of their children in South Africa. With schooling so integral to how one eventually turns out; it must indeed be reassuring that any community, in the face of potentially falling standards in the future, can potentially collaborate with like-minded individuals and organisations to create a bespoke education environment for their kids.

In many other societies without any legislation comparable to the South African Schools Act of 1996, parents must simply like it or lump it. Here, as is usual practice across so many sectors, if the citizen does not like what they see, they are almost always permitted to collaborate, seek permission and create.

There's more that's become quite kiff in the South African education sector. From the old talk shop PTAs (Parent Teacher Associations), parents of South African school-going children are now guaranteed by the Schools Act to have a say in the running of public schools. This is due to the national policy on state schools requiring that the school governing body (SGB) be made up of management, teachers and even learners - at least at the high school level.

Eons ago when the developed world seemed to be improving in so many positive ways every passing year, it was kak when the British tourist would make that usual remark about South Africa being 'ten years behind the UK'. Ten years behind the UK, or the rest of the first world for that matter, was kak when we were watching TV1.

Today, when I'm told South Africa is 10 years behind x or y country that seems to be so 'advanced', they've forgotten the basics, I think 'yes, please!'. In a post-pandemic, climate change world where much of what was formerly coveted now seems so superfluous to any thinking person, much of that overseas so-called progress just doesn't seem quite so appealing anymore. The less said about that the better and you can read between the lines.

My view on education in South Africa is a simple one. With a population of 60m people, there will always be an enormous chunk of like-minded parents very interested in ensuring quality education remains available for their children. In fact, a fixed-wireless connection or a mobile base station delivering high-speed data is (almost) all one needs nowadays to receive a decent education. I put the 'almost' there to pacify my children's teachers who are fantastic, South African government school educators and irreplaceable by bits and bytes.

In the final analysis, whether that school down the road is a gem in the community or a lump of coal that blights the whole neighbourhood actually depends less on government and more on us. Involved parents produce evolved schools. It's not very fair to say all communities get the schools they deserve, but when it comes to middle class neighbourhoods with parents who have the time and resources to throw at the local school, there's no excuse for a kak government school in a kiff South African neighbourhood.

We remain fortunate to have a government that permits a mix of public, independent, alternative learning schools such as Waldorf and Montessori, international and home school approaches to schooling.

We are lucky government also permits schools to develop their own mixed sources of funding. There is clear education oversight in South Africa, but also a lot of scope for independent creativity and excellence in schools here. This means many SA schools, for all intents and purposes, are blank slates onto which local communities can carve promising futures for their kids.

That's not all. We can top the education pudding off with pervasive fibre and high-speed wireless Internet that enables a sprinkle of further innovations such as online high schools of which UCT Online High School (modelled after Stanford University Online High School) is the best example, offering both SA National Senior Certificate and Cambridge international qualifications.

By the way, the proof - as always - is in the pudding. The multi-flavoured kids pouring out of South African schools generally look happy and I've never heard anyone here comment on how afraid they are to walk past a group of South African school kids.

Any parent in South Africa today who claims to be worried about the future of their children and specifically trots out 'just look at the education system' is embarrassingly behind the times and sadly allowing stereotypes and outdated predictions to get the better of them. They need to update their thinking and, as I have said elsewhere in this book, the future already happened.

There are a vast array of education options on offer within a multi-faceted South African education system that provides exceptional value for money to boot. What's more - and I love this part as much as our happy South African twins do - in many schools here, shoes are optional.

16

Now Gender-Based Progress is a Thing

It was kak when we would proudly read our progressive constitution which admirably says 'the state may not unfairly discriminate directly or indirectly against anyone on one or more grounds, including race, gender, sex, pregnancy, marital status, ethnic or social origin, colour, sexual orientation, age, disability, religion, conscience, belief, culture, language and birth' – and then we'd be dismayed to hear about daily violence directed at LGBTQI people.

No-one is suggesting that gender-based violence has gone on holiday in Moscow, but did we ever think we'd walk into a Checkers, Woolies, Clicks or Pick 'n Pay store and be greeted by a smiling transgender person at the till nobody klapped?

South Africa's gone way more liberal than anyone expected and this tolerance is palpably being felt in city centres, townships and suburbs across a country that formerly flung sexuality-based slurs at anyone who didn't clutch their Lion Lager with quite the expected gusto. Yes, there's a long way to go, but I don't miss those conservative days when shorts were short and socks were itchy.

South Africa is the only country in sub-Saharan Africa that permits same-sex marriages. This recent quote from the UK's Financial Times is quite an eye-opener: "In some ways, South Africa, an upper-middle-income economy, a democracy and a heavy carbon emitter, has more in common with the global north than the global south."

There's gender-based progress everywhere in South Africa and yet none of this is noted by parents 'worried about the future'. You're worried about the future and you're off to a country where the drinking culture means its sexual assault Friday and physical assault Saturday?

As much as South Africa is a traditionally conservative society, no-one has ever walked into a gay club here and shot the place up. The fact we're making progress in protecting and, indeed, advancing women and vulnerable members of society (and abortion remains legal here) is something to consider when pondering the future of one's children who may well not live the same lifestyle as you nor make the same choices. It's kiff that South Africa continues to put distance between herself and that bigoted past, emerging every day more tolerant.

Much of South Africa has become so laid back to the point where even gogo's eyebrows are not raised when the latest LGBTQI character makes an appearance on her favourite soapie.

17

Public Transport Works – Even if it's Private

The availability of public transport in South Africa has done a complete and most kiff 180.

Curiously, however, few of us who used to trot out 'there's no public transport in this country' appear to now acknowledge that getting around South Africa's towns and cities has become a non-issue.

From about ten percent of the population (urban mostly white South Africans) having easy access to hundreds of metered taxis a few decades ago, we now have the pleasant situation where about 90% of the population (everyone in major to mid-sized cities and towns with mobile coverage) has ready access to the thousands of sedan taxis in the employ of Uber, Bolt and similar.

For the millions of us who live close to where we work, play and receive an education, it's cheaper to use ride-share services than own a car. So this emergence of a new kind of tech-based public transport - in South Africa - is a big thing that just didn't exist before. As an aside, it's plainly wrong to claim that ride-share somehow doesn't count in the realm of local transport.

The point bears repeating because you may not be aware of the never-mentioned fact that the access to Uber and others that South Africans routinely enjoy is not guaranteed everywhere in the world.

What? Yes, when you say that Uber and similar services somehow don't count as SA public transport systems (do they transport, um, the public, for a small fee?) because every country has them, you're clearly unaware that Uber and its competitors are not guaranteed to be available everywhere.

We're fortunate our government allows rideshare services in South African cities like Cape Town, Joburg, Pretoria and Putsonderwater; because they don't have them in Copenhagen.

Really? Yes, and in Canada, for instance, Uber has repeatedly run into trouble and it's only available in a limited number of municipalities. There's no chance of requesting an Uber in Switzerland, nor China, and you can likewise forget about it in Thailand or Turkey and, as we saw above, in first-world Denmark too. There are 195 countries in the world and almost two-thirds of them do not have Uber.

So the availability of public transport in South Africa is today a lot more efficient thanks to the ride-share services that every South African province permits. South Africa's better-than-world-class cellular networks, and above average cellular penetration, also enable Uber and others to function optimally. The reason Uber works so well here is because mobile works so well here.

I do understand that equating Uber with a public transport system might be 'problematic', at least for those of us who have been led to believe that multi-occupant (and I do mean multi) mass transit systems are the ideal way of moving people.

Mass transit systems move people out of necessity, not because clunkety clunk is how we really all want to get around. Since when did moving people in metal boxes at high speed become an aspirational thing? Most people in the world would choose to walk out into the South African sunshine and hop in a ride-share over getting sopping wet before being slam dunked into a tube of unfriendlies.

Many South Africans have been wide-eyed with excitement during that first mass transit ride in some or other overseas city. Fabulous soon turns to 'F$#% this sucks – I wish I was in an Uber going to after work drinks in Camps Bay / Parkhurst'.

I ignore those 'most liveable cities' indexes because the young hairies who compile that predictable nonsense don't know what a Highveld climate is and place a premium on railways like Victoria's still on the throne bullying the boers. Oh, do let me guess – the world's best city to live in is... Vancouver. Or did exciting Oslo reclaim the top spot this year?

Like Winston Churchill found out (see 'boers' above), we have many trains that don't run on time in South Africa. We have some that are on time and some that time forgot, but then, it's the 21st century and there's an Uber three minutes away.

BTW, if you're in Joburg and can't wait three minutes for an Uber, BRT buses depart every three minutes at peak times. Outside of peak times, it's every three weeks. I'm joking. See? Let's have a jol as we perk ourselves up by realising that things are not nearly as kak as you thought in Mzansi.

Anti-train propaganda aside, the emergence of the 10 Gautrain stations around Joburg has been an incredible leap forward for transport in South Africa and it's a leap that seems to now be taken for granted as our attention focuses less on how to get around.

Let's, however, not forget how kak it was not too long ago when the only way to get from Sandton to OR Tambo was by agreeing to a metered taxi driver virtually mugging you for over an hour in broad daylight as you sat in his comfy back seat.

We've now been exposed to the Ubers and trains of the varied and accessible South African transport system that has improved enormously when measured by the objective question: 'Can I stand on the nearest street corner and get a ride?'. When I was growing up, getting around was difficult. Few middling types outside of UCT academia ventured into the minibus taxis that were starting to make an appearance – mostly out of the fear that comes with entrusting your life to a spanner-steered Toyota.

Today, my goodness, where did all those dodgy taxis with their multi-coloured panels go? Government put its foot down, and in came the Taxi Recapitalisation Programme. Since 2006, this initiative has been a huge success and has seen the scrapping of over 81 000 old bangers and their replacement by decent-looking Toyota Quantums that are now the de facto, fairly respectable centrepieces of South African mass transport.

Now, I really can stand at the nearest corner and get a safe and comfortable ride. Indeed, it feels like sometimes I could actually swing my feet off my bed in the morning and be immediately scooped up by a flying white taxi festooned with that SA flag logo that appropriately appears to be a nod to Halley's Comet. The taxi industry still has a long way to go, but no-one can deny it has smartened itself up. Yes, there's often a taxi strike on the go. However, as the mass impounding of vehicles by the authorities indicates, the taxi industry is no longer an untouchable mob.

I think we'll end off now because transport as a subject really is - to be honest - not all that kiff. Some countries elevate their mass transit systems to the status of tourist attraction because, well, that's all they've got. Yes, I did have to drive my car past that porcupine early this morning because there's no train where I live, but I saw a porcupine – on the way to that beach... that has the penguins.

I've hardly mentioned the Bus Rapid Transit (BRT) systems that South Africa has rolled out across a number of cities. Take it from my cousin, BRT works. Here, take it from the World Bank (2022) also: "With bus rapid transit, African cities are riding towards a better future."

In the final analysis, things are indeed getting closer and more convenient in South Africa. Now anyone can take a tuk-tuk to Sandton, an Uber to Alberton, a Gaubus to Garsfontein and a BRT to Braamfontein. None of these options was available just a few Presidents ago.

18

SA Sport Returns to the Locker Room

Sport was used to divide us in the bad old days (mostly rugby for me, mostly soccer for you) and then used as a force for reconciliation in those Mandela-era dreamy days.

Today, as the big picture slowly gets better in South Africa - like an elephant steadily getting its A into G as it rises to its feet - more integrated, more representative sport has become so normal in this country that we scarcely notice.

Yes, there is still much to be done, but what's the sub-title of this book? "South Africa's Getting Better". Getting better – exactly. A work in progress with progress for sure.

If we want to talk about progress, and progress tinged with excellence at that, one only has to take a gander at some of the surnames of the heroes who gave the All Blacks their biggest ever thrashing in history: Kolisi,

Arendse, Marx, Mbonambi and Smith. A rainbow nation indeed!

We cheer, we cry, we rant and rave from our stadium seats, lounge suites and passenger seats – does any South African sports fan ever halt the emotion to stop and think about the complexion of the hero giving their all before them? Please. That's for places where they have yet to embark on reconciliation.

Do you remember how kiff it was in the 90s when we first spotted Oberholzer in Accounts wearing his first ever Bafana Bafana shirt at the company year end function? Then Buthelezi upstairs started signalling his support for the Boks and today the vast majority of South Africans only see the national colours above, and who cares about the skin tones below? I'm not mad about sport, but I am fanatical about this country and the reconciliation now baked into our national identity.

This, however, is not a short diversion into the power of sport to bring us together. We know about Mandela Magic and our rainbow past. Even the Millennials and Gen Z have seen those glorious images of Mandela and Francois Pienaar celebrating the Springboks' 1995 Rugby World Cup victory.

These 600 sports-centred words, thin on facts yet heavy on common sense, are placed here to drive home the kiff point that an enormous amount of work has been done, memorandums of understanding negotiated, milestones achieved or in-progress so that, today, South African spectator sport is good quality, guilt-free and light on action-distracting sideshows.

In this decade, the sports fan gets to experience the work that has gone into keeping South African sports world-class while embarking on necessary transformation. South African sport is indeed getting better. It has largely dispensed with the baggage of the past and this has enabled all of us to enjoy what's on offer in our, mostly unified sports-mad country. Many of the teething issues that so often played out in the media around integration have been dealt with - or are being dealt with in a respectful way - leaving the fans able to focus on their passion.

The fair and representative way forward has been set. Debates around symbols, quotas, and more are now accepted agenda items as the country emerges stronger and better for dealing with them.

Now, South Africans can gather around the braai and enjoy a few pretentious lite beers as drama-lite becomes the new normal in local sport. We're not there yet, but it's onwards and upwards in SA sport.

If we must have facts to back up sentiment, try this one: The 2020 Tokyo Summer Olympics saw South Africa send its biggest-ever squad who participated in the majority of sporting codes. Yes, biggest ever. Some 30 years after democracy, the Republic of South Africa fielded its biggest-ever Olympic team.

19

The Party's on in this State

The party is the state and the state is the party. That's a kak state of affairs that was closer to materialising in South Africa when the ANC was a two-thirds-plus party. Today's watered-down ANC is a lot more kiff for the goal of a successful South Africa that needs diversity of thought as much as diversity of ethnicity.

South Africa has progressed to the point where the state is not necessarily the party and the party is not necessarily the state. In fact, it's quite likely the official in front of you is either an opposition supporter or apolitical and simply doing their job.

South Africa is not and will never be a Zimbabwe. Firstly, the Constitution is the touchstone of state power in South Africa. Power does not emanate from any individual political party. Secondly, cadre deployment (party functionaries given state jobs to entrench party rule) has been struck down by the High Court as illegal. Thirdly, the Public Protector is constitutionally an independent seat of highly-effective prosecutorial power dedicated to preserving the South African democratic state. It is this impartial office that brought state capture to a grinding halt. Fourthly, while it does occasionally happen, the use of state resources for electioneering is a known no-no in South Africa, even by the most dyed-in-the-wool party supporter. Like corruption, brazenly engaging in the former activity is becoming increasingly frowned upon in society and subject to sanctions.

All of this prevents the conflation of party and state. If we want to talk about blurred lines, we should look further north at the example of America and how its president has a starring role in the nomination of all new judges of the Supreme Court. What can you expect from the world's leading fauxmocracy and its two-party system?

When people smarter than myself refer to 'checks and balances' built into the South African multiparty system, they are referring to the separation of powers between the legislature, executive and judiciary.

According to the Constitutional Court: "The legislature (parliament, the provincial legislatures and local councils) makes the laws and monitors the executive; the executive (the president, deputy president and ministers) makes policy, proposes laws and implements laws passed by the legislature; and the judiciary tries cases and administers justice."

Every part of this proven system keeps the other in check. This balanced system is a cornerstone of every successful democracy in the world.

According to Hugh Corder in The Conversation: "... from 1948 to 1994, the executive arm of government dominated over parliament. At the start of the new democratic era, the drafters of the 1996 Constitution changed this. The constitution gives the legislature the authority and the obligation to oversee the exercise of public power, and hold the executive accountable. The constitution contains nearly 40 provisions to do this."

With South Africa's liberation movement now reduced to a more encouraging and democracy-boosting simple majority in Parliament, it's kiff that the pervasive conflation of party and state can reliably be left out of the South African scenario handbook.

In any event, the ANC is not Zimbabwe's Zanu-PF, Angola's MPLA or Mozambique's Frelimo. It set itself on a different course and we can see this by its actions and the ANC's 2012 "Organisational Renewal" document.

Rays of sunlight permeate the text. The paper claims "the ANC has learnt from the experiences of other liberation movements and progressive parties". The mere fact this document exists means some learning has indeed taken place.

Mondli Makhanya, writing on TimesLive.co.za about this first attempt at renewal, says: "Another aspect which should not be taken lightly is the recognition by the ANC that it could lose power one day. For the ANC to understand this and begin to sensitise its members is a big step."

This impressive quote deserves to be dusted off and again put out there to remind us that the ANC has already realised it cannot go down a path that would end the party for everyone. Cheers to that!

20

It's Kiff Now we are Learning Our Own Rules

The World Justice Project (WJP) evaluates the rule of law in 139 countries and, in its first report since the Covid-19 pandemic, placed South Africa at 8th position out of 40 upper middle income countries.

SA's global rule of law ranking stayed static. The WJP, however, noted "multiyear negative trends" across the rest of the world. So while many South Africans continue to labour under the erroneous impression that it's all becoming wild here, actually respect for the law in South Africa remains within the first cohort amongst nations with a fair amount of dosh.

There used to be 'petty apartheid' here and now petty little laws characterise life in much of the developed world.

This morning, I experienced a bit of a parallel parking palava and, upon my return, noticed I had parked my car a little too far from the kerb. I remember a time when a traffic cop would emerge and fine you for being some arbitrary number of centimetres too far from the pavement. I'm glad that petty little South Africa has emigrated. I think it's sensible focusing on licence discs and roadworthiness instead.

People talk a lot of rubbish about South Africa. Haven't we all heard about corruption being 'endemic' here? What a load of nonsense. Do you know what 'endemic' means? It means you can get exactly nothing done without the daily greasing of palms. In countries rotten to the core, everything runs on the hard cash that every citizen must pocket before even thinking of leaving home.

Ordinary South Africans going about their daily business do not regularly and routinely bribe the traffic police, tax authorities, municipal workers, licensing clerks, postal employees and other minor functionaries to get anything done. That's when corruption is 'endemic'. It means nothing moves forward until money is paid and that is clearly not the case in South Africa. My monthly admin items get quite nicely resolved with polite emails. No one expects a brown paper bag under the bridge at midnight. Come on, keep it real.

The rubbish collectors sheepishly asking for a 'Christmas Box' once a year, for instance, is hardly a symptom of 'endemic' corruption and, actually, quite a nice little tradition that speaks to a culturally supreme place. There are splashes of interestingness woven throughout our diverse, rule-of-law-based society.

If Prince William were one of us, he might say: "We are very much not an endemically corrupt country." A country that ranks 8th amongst middle income countries for the rule of law is also very much not even close to being a 'failed state'.

I wasn't going to include any mention of this lazy idea in this book, but it must be dealt with. This term is the current shock value darling of the local media and so many mediocre opinion pages commentators who bandy it around without comprehending the own goal they're scoring for South Africa, themselves and their children. Shameful.

The 'failed state' brigade is the latest incarnation of those who would like nothing better than to say "we told you so" when it comes to South Africa. In their world view; North America is awesome, South America is corrupt, Europe is progress, Asia is confusion and Africa is war. That's how most of the world and the world's press sees it and they must have totally wet themselves when the shells flew in South Africa from 1899 to 1902.

I have a pet theory that at least some of the over-the-top negativity launched at South Africa is institutionally-based and emanates directly from British journalists reporting on the thrashing their troops regularly received at the Southern tip of Africa.

Clearly, nothing good could come from such a place and this jaundiced view continues to the present day. When on holiday, the Brits love the sights and sounds of South Africa. When behind their keyboards, it's another story and forgive the pun.

Admittedly, they gave us a break in the 1990s when it was realised Madiba Magic could sell as many newspapers as Civil War, but now the agendas are back as the same tired old twak is written and posted about South Africa. It's always way over the top and seldom gels with what's actually happening on the ground. For instance, far from us all having such little respect for the rule of law, there is a decided shift towards respect for the everyday laws that govern our daily behaviour.

We see this, for example, in much less tolerance now for drink driving. It's no joke to say driving drunk in South Africa used to be a national sport. I can remember when the manne around the braai would joke about how hammered they were when they got into the car last week. Terrible. We were all used to drinking as much as we liked and then zig-zagging home with abandon.

Today, most groups of friends would not dare boast to each other how drunk they've been behind the wheel. Not only has the drink driving limit been reduced from 0.08g to 0.05g of alcohol per 100 millilitres of blood (for professional drivers, the limit is 0.02g), but most South Africans would agree that roadblocks today are more visible, better resourced and more effective. IOL reported recently how a single roadblock in Pretoria netted over 1 000 wanted suspects!

When it comes to defective vehicles and adherence to roadworthiness rules, South Africa used to be a place where you could drive around with that cracked windscreen until the car itself fell apart. It's very difficult to get away with an obviously unroadworthy vehicle today. Take a gander at the first couple of dozen cars lined up at your nearest shopping mall parking lot. You'll be hard-pressed to spot an expired license disc between them.

Tax compliance, too, is an area where South Africans are falling into line and respecting the rules. Doesn't the entire nation know when it's tax season? We'll quickly deal with another key fallacy about South Africa. The doomers and gloomers would have us believe that, to put it in a very tidy nutshell, all the country's taxpayers are emigrating. More naysayer nonsense. In fact, the 2022/2023 financial year saw SARS collect an all-time high of R1.69 trillion.

SARS also collected 8.3% more - not less - personal income tax compared to the previous tax year and added a substantial 1.17m new personal income tax payers to the country's personal income tax base of just under 26m people. Yes, few of those new taxpayers immediately started paying tax as most currently earn below the required threshold, but hundreds of thousands of South Africans proactively registering for tax and getting a tax number speaks to both law-abiding and upwardly-mobile. Now, for ready reference for the benefit of the misinformed, there are about 4.5m white people in total in SA. I'm just putting that in there to make the obvious point that it's been much less about us for some time now.

There's also the fact that personal income tax makes up just 35% of South Africa's total tax receipts. A quarter is made up of Value-Added Tax (which all 60m consumers pay) and one-fifth is made up of corporate tax. This is a good mix. South Africa, for the foreseeable future, will clearly remain a middle upper income country and it really no longer matters if all of Sea Point relocates to a new Promenade.

If we return to our original focus about the rule of law in South Africa, there are many other examples where citizens and the law intersect on a daily basis and where there has been improvement in compliance.

Most South Africans in relationships know that the SAPS, the courts, and society at large now have an extremely low tolerance for domestic violence. Lift a hand to your partner and there's every chance you'll be in the cells. This is a massive departure from that former South Africa where klaps were routinely dished out in the home and everywhere else.

From practically no legislative framework, today we have the Domestic Violence Act 116 of 1998 which amongst others, formalised the Protection Order and set us on the path towards quashing this horrible form of abuse.

This is how the SAPS deals with domestic violence in a South Africa getting better: "If there is reason to believe that an act of violence has been committed, the respondent must be arrested immediately without a warrant. Search the premises and seize for safekeeping any firearms and/or dangerous weapons." Sounds good to me!

Interestingly, Statistics South Africa released a 2021 report saying that 21% of women in South Africa had experienced physical violence by a partner. This is lower than the global rate of 27% of women aged 15 to 49 in a relationship reporting physical and/or sexual violence by their partner, according to Integrated Emergency Response (iER).

We can go on and on about the clamping down on maintenance dodgers, fraudsters, owners of illegal and unregistered weapons and so on. But why? It should now be obvious from the above that there are indeed rules in South Africa and they are enforced, perhaps not all the time, but most of the time.

Quite frankly, who wants to live in a soul-crushing society where compliance is vigorous, petty and total and could be said to affect the law-abiding citizen as much as the criminal?

21

First There Were Four Now There Are More

The discovery of a gold reef on the farm Langlaagte saw Johannesburg established as a small village in 1886. Today; Joburg, Jozi or eGoli, is the undisputed maker of fortunes in South Africa.

Just over 13 decades old, this nouveau riche upstart is emerging as one of the 50 largest urban agglomerations in the world. It's also credited with being the world's most treed city. That alone is incredibly kiff when one takes a moment to appreciate the birdlife and birdsong that accompanies the world's greenest cityscape.

So when a city becomes so big and so green at the same time, delivering so much for so many, why then do we swoop down from the bigger picture, reach for the microscope and pontificate about the decline of some of the inner city?

Bemoaning the fate of Hillbrow, for example, while languishing at a ritzy café in the 'New North' which didn't even exist until fairly recently, that's like bemoaning the loss of the VW Beetle while driving a BMW.

Actually, I think I'd prefer the Beetle. But most people wouldn't and you get where I'm going. This pattern of the fall of one area and the rise of another is repeated in communities countrywide, indeed, worldwide.

In any event, Hillbrow and other neighbourhoods that experienced periods of 1990s-era decline are far from lost causes.

Take this recent reporting from Joburg.org.za: "Various stakeholders collaborated with the city and Pikitup to spruce up the streets of Hillbrow. They cleared illegal dumping sites, swept streets and planted trees. They included the National Department of Forestry, Fisheries and Environment, Gauteng Department of Agriculture and Rural Development, Dotted O Foundation, Clean City SA, SAPS Hillbrow, Ekhaya Environmental Group, Rand Clinic, Reef Hotel and Mzansi FM Radio. They all pledged their support for the city's War on Waste campaign."

I bet the SAPS is the only name above you recognised. That's because a lot of kiff initiatives involving people and organisations you've never heard of do cool stuff in South African cities getting better every day. Only consuming formulaic, click-driven news from the usual media platforms means we miss a lot of what's really happening around South Africa.

We're in desperate need of more media choice. I, for one, am tired of reading that attention-grabbing, semi-truthful and very negative headline, moving on in the first few paragraphs (the only ones actually read – damage done) to a sensational story designed to scare the wits out of anyone planning to stay in South Africa, and then burying the truth in softer language towards the end (that no-one reads – damage done) to cover the writer against allegations of overly-negative, untruthful reporting.

This style of plainly-obvious, South Africa-bashing journalism does no-one any good and certainly doesn't motivate anyone to fix anything in South Africa. Does anybody feel like doing anything good to make things better after being told how kak they are? Sadly, instead of pulling together for the common good, every generation has their Lord Haw Haws stuffing it up for the rest of us.

I digress, once again, but only because I've just got off the web after digesting the usual drivel about South Africa on this Saturday morning. It upsets me no end and that's because there are serious, real-world outcomes to year after year of 'South Africa = doom and gloom' reporting. It's also so boring. How many more times must they cry wolf?

Let's get back to the facts. The moon waxes and wanes and so do the fortunes of neighbourhoods within every city that's ever risen from the earth. One neighbourhood experiences a period of falling property values, high crime and vacancies, and another neighbourhood - often perplexingly close by - experiences rocketing property values and a crush at the pavement cafe coffee counter as the smuglies pile in with their low-mileage North Face attire.

It's kak when you overhear those conversations about former cosmopolitan city centre neighbourhoods around the country falling on hard times. But it's kiff when you understand that urban decay is a thing experienced by all world cities.

Nobody, nothing and certainly no neighbourhood rides the crest forever. Fortunately, as we see in the smidgen of an illustrative example above, South Africa is fortunate in that things are not simply allowed to fall into an endless pit of disrepair.

Haven't you noticed that in South Africa, there always seems to be a point beyond which we will not go? We see buildings being turned around, parks painted, streets fixed and pavements beautified. Then we get on Whatsapp to next door with 'Hey, did you see, two trucks arrived with council workers and they fixed the playground?'. This happens a lot and not only on Mandela Day. Incidentally, another amazing legacy of the great man that sees much kak turned to kiff every 18 July.

I started this chapter wanting to emphasize the important fact that everyone appears to miss when, specifically, mentioning the H-word in a negative sense. Yes, Hillbrow went kak. But we gained the transformation of Sandton which went on to become the richest square mile of a whole continent! Of course, Joburg's new suburbs or rather, the reinvention of formerly rural areas, goes way beyond Sandton.

There is not a single undeveloped parcel of land along the N1 from Joburg to Pretoria. How on earth can anyone, in all seriousness, say Joburg and Gauteng are on the decline in the face of that level of development? That's just being ignorant.

Ever since I was a kid, I've been told how kak Joburg is, and yet: 'thar she blows'! Still shining, still growing and still a destination for fortune seekers. I'm a beach Booth, by the way, but I fell in love with Joburg the first time I drove into town at sunset in 1999 and the grass down the N1 was on fire. It was like entering the gates of hell and I loved it.

Time has not stood still in South Africa's money, trees and fabulous weather heartland where human beings continue to build, and build, and build. Former residents of Johannesburg would be hard-pressed to navigate the many new suburban and commercial areas that seem to mushroom ever closer together and yet burst outwards at the same time. The same is true right across the length and breadth of the country.

Wasn't the South Africa we first knew the sum total of Johannesburg, Cape Town, Pretoria, Durban and Port Elizabeth? If you were being generous, you might add East London and Bloemfontein to the list of the country's major towns and cities. Today, the choice of where to live and pursue business or study opportunities is extensive. South Africa's list of kiff towns and cities has definitely gotten a lot more interesting.

So many new developments now exist. We already referred to the semigration phenomenon that's seeing dozens of small towns around South Africa serve much better coffee. There are loads of these up-and-comers – nine, in particular, are mentioned in the 2022 Africa Wealth Report as already being established and popular with high net wealth individuals: Hermanus, Paarl, Franschhoek, Stellenbosch, Umhlanga, La Lucia, Ballito, Plettenberg Bay, Knysna, George and Wilderness. All of the latter are outstanding – why cross continents to live well when you can cross provinces?

According to the Mail & Guardian, there are also numerous 'smart cities' springing up around South Africa that use technology and data to improve efficiencies and quality of life. Of course, every South African knows that quality of life actually depends on a hot fire, burnt meat and tipsy friends. But we'll indulge our much-needed nerds.

Some examples of state-of-the-art urban developments already being built include African Coastal Smart City (between Port St John's and Margate), Nkosi City (Bordering the Kruger National Park in Mpumalanga), Mooikloof Mega City (Pretoria) and Lanseria Smart City (clearly, living near a compact international airport is a very smart move). None of this is pie in the sky. We haven't even got to new private sector-led settlements like Steyn City, Waterfall City and others. A headline last year in TechCentral noted: "SA is well-positioned to accelerate the move to smart cities".

These lists above are obviously not exhaustive – they serve merely to point out that bricks and mortar-based improvement is happening in your suburb, in your town and in our South Africa. Please bear with us.

22

My Gatehouse is Kiffer Than Yours

Switched-on South Africans know it's not about the facts. It's all about semantics, stereotypes and sentiment.

We know this because we see how 0.4% GDP growth in a developed country after a negative quarterly performance is called a 'bounce-back'. South Africa will do the same economically and be said to be 'escaping a technical recession'. It's not growth, they suggest, it's almost not growth. It's all so predictable. To be happy in SA, adopt a 'meh' approach when you read how kak it's supposed to be here. Then go for a walk and seethe as I do. I can't help it.

Forget how we're doing, the same negativity trails where we live. Prince Harry lives in a 'gated community', an aspirational place, right? South Africans live in 'secure complexes', on virtual pain of death, apparently, and definitely not aspirational. Except, now they are.

South Africa's secure complexes with their strands of electrified wire atop high walls and always featuring a gatehouse and boom at the entrance were an invention born out of necessity as crime escalated in the 1990s. They became as much a magnet for local families as foreign journalists who could not zoom in close enough to those yellow warning signs. One could sense the disappointment when they arrived thinking an electric fence was something out of 'Lost' and not, simply, four strands of wire.

Never mind, it's back to the Hyatt or the Michelangelo as said journo predictably interviews South Africa's most pessimistic Uber driver about the only topics his Cambridge-educated producer could come up with for an African country: crime and corruption. Then it's a superb steak, a superior sunset and some African fiction. The hack is, of course, writing the fiction, not reading it. My goodness, this is a major diversion even for me.

Kiffly enough, the entrance of complexes onto the residential housing scene came at the right time as they helped solved growing crime, densification and affordability challenges all at once. South African suburbs were previously characterised by large, single-dwelling plots that created the problem of urban sprawl, never mind the problem of how to sleep soundly at night: because the pool pump's sucking air again – what did you think?

Today, the 'complex' has morphed into the 'estate' and it's become much less about security and more about swish. There's also a heavy emphasis on sustainability with nature incorporated instead of obliterated. And fortunately, someone else does the pool.

I think we all saw this coming when it became clear South Africa was not going to implode, home security became just a thing like Wi-Fi, and developers started adding wine cellars, concierge services, chip and putt courses, nature walks, the odd buck and peacock, rooftop entertainment areas, and so much more besides to the South African gated living experience.

We've also seen a much smarter, more low-key approach to complex security and this has increased their attractiveness.

So it was kak when we thought we were being herded into group living for our own security in the 90s and kiff when that herding turned to 'oh, there are not one, but two peacocks on my stoep. I must order not one, but two bottles from the cellar.'

Not only have South Africa's complexes, estates, gated communities or thee and four-star working and middle class lockups made the transition from necessary to aspirational with a heavy dollop of convenience on the side; they've slid so easily into their new niche as the perfect housing option for the entertainer whose more budget-friendly complex unit looks a lot more impressive to the wannabes than a comparably-priced residential home.

For those of us keen to explore this 'world in one country' our parents told us about, the complex unit is very likely to be securely in place with not a brick, geyser, house sitter or pricey chocolate-coloured Labrador missing upon our return. And for those who just can't do 'fixer-upper', the complex is the ideal way to get onto the housing ladder (often without a deposit or transfer duties – another plus of living in SA) and actually make a profit later on (another plus of living in SA) without having to get onto an actual scary ladder.

This profit point that snuck in above is quite important. I was going to write at length about how much easier it is to get into the South African housing market, and do well out of it, without having to ask one's parents for the deposit or live at home saving for it until you're just ripe for a 55-plus assisted living estate.

Alas, I'm on a deadline with this book. So what I will present in passing here is the anecdotal evidence I've amassed in my misfiring brain that seems to point to the fact that making a profit in property is not guaranteed worldwide. In South Africa, it virtually is. Considering that one's home is, for most people, the biggest financial commitment they'll ever make, it's kiff that in South Africa, you really have to buy a lemon to mess up a property investment.

I'd never heard of 'negative equity' (or three mortgages on one home) until American sitcoms enlightened me. And then two close relatives recently had to sell their home in Europe at a loss. I've overheard that overseas residential property implosion story at least a few times while sitting at Fish Hoek's finest, low-priced coffee shops. It's safe to say that for most South African salary earners, the most money they've ever made has been due to property.

Now, related to the 'birds on the balcony' that we were introduced briefly to above are 'kids in the complex'. Let me explain.

Complex living was about not being murdered. Let's be honest. Now that most of us appreciate the remoteness (even in South Africa) of the ultimate in stranger danger, we can focus on the fact that a happy by-product of living in Fort Knox is that the South African gated community kids are now safer than the kids with the funny accent in Ramsay Street. This is because secure complexes solve both the problem of the murdering madman and the growing global issue of the uncle in the ice cream truck.

23

South Africans Join the Dots From Graft to Glory

South Africa's 60m-plus people are today better educated than they've ever been and highly motivated by both hustle and start-up culture.

Forget first world debates around work-life balance, it's kiff that South Africans want to progress and are embracing education and aspiration.

While millions hit the books under trying conditions, the naysayers will simply dismiss this mass education of a nation, preferring instead to point to failings in South Africa's education system. I'll point them to people who are themselves failing - failing to see the wood for the trees.

In South Africa we know there are wealthy, functional schools and we know there are poorly-funded, dysfunctional schools. However, Matthew Sterne, writing in the Mail & Guardian in 2021 notes the two most important facts when it comes to education in South Africa: "more learners are in school than ever before" and "South Africa invests a considerable amount of our GDP in education."

When it comes to literacy, a 2023 report by the World Literacy Foundation that says just 4.7% of South Africans have low-level literacy. That doesn't sound too bad. Unless you're one of the 4.7%. What I will say is, be a little circumspect when reading news reports of large numbers of SA primary school kids being unable to 'read for meaning'. What isn't mentioned in these doom and gloom articles is these unfortunate kids are being tested in English! Let me ask you to read a paragraph in Swahili and see how well you do.

The annually-issued report 'Education at a Glance: OECD Countries' is called the 'authoritative source of information on the state of education around the world.

This document echoes the above when it says 'more adults are attaining upper secondary education in South Africa than a decade ago' and continues with 'the country spends a larger share of its wealth on the public funding of primary, secondary and post secondary non-tertiary education than most OECD and partner countries.'

We're all familiar with South Africa's high unemployment figures. However, the above report notes the encouraging fact that 'tertiary education pays off in South Africa' because 85% of South Africans with tertiary qualifications are employed.

It's interesting, then, that most of the people who are the first to complain about their future prospects and that of their kids, are actually 85% immune from being unemployed in South Africa.

Backing up the encouraging fact that more South Africans attend school than ever before is the fairly recent research by Cambridge International which found that 85% (ditto) of South African students aspire to continue their studies at university once they have left school.

Let me run that past you again. Some 85% of young South African school leavers do not aspire to be rappers or embark on a 'gap year' at their parents' expense. No, the enormous majority of young people in a country that spends most of its money on education want to be educated. This is totally in line with former days when we would read about that number one dream of the majority of South Africans when we started transitioning to a democracy: sending one's kids to a 'Model C' school.

It's kiff that the stars are aligning for South Africa because she has her priorities right. It's also interesting to note that a quick web search reveals that for every 100 students studying locally, four South African students are equipping themselves overseas. From a formerly closed South Africa, a statistic like this illustrates South Africa's growing interest, reach and involvement with the world.

You can't move upwards and onwards without a dream. I often think of the young South Africans I meet as mini Martin Luther Kings in the making because they all seem to have a dream and a roadmap of how to get there.

Young people wanting to achieve is a good thing and it's the reason I mentioned 'hustle culture' in the opening line above. Before hustle culture, the grind and start-ups became a thing, South Africans of a certain sort would whine about everybody wanting 'handouts'.

It's not worth elaborating here but, suffice to say, those days – if they did exist – are over. South Africans today celebrate hustle culture and the grind as the way to get ahead in their careers. Young people in this country are not afraid of hard work.

Ask a group of 20-somethings what they do for a living and I bet most would have their fingers in multiple pies – not because, as in the US, it's impossible for so many singletons to survive on one income – but because South Africans are ambitious, natural-born movers and shakers and always in a hurry.

How did we get the laid back label? I find it's quite the opposite. South Africans are always off on their next mission, and it's either something they're building, studying or starting.

So many have their eye on their own business as the end result of what people in other countries would call 'burnout culture'. Stars burn, coal glows. I'm happy our future's burning brighter powered by our young superstars; their work ethic, and their growing interest in enabling technologies.

When the sum total of mobile technology amounted to SMS, voicemail, ringtones and downloads, those annual surveys revealing South Africans to be the world's biggest users of text messages were just signalling the start of the GDP-boosting love affair with mobile technology that was to come.

South Africa long ago exceeded the 100% mobile penetration rate with many of us owning multiple mobile devices. That initial desire to own a cellphone in the 1990s has morphed into a full-on total love affair with technology of all types.

We see this in the explosion of coding in South Africa. I grew up in a South Africa where everyone wanted to be in marketing. Today it's coding. That's very good for South Africa's global competitiveness. It's also very good for these future coders as 40% of current South African coders are based here earning dollars and euros, says BusinessTech, while enjoying family and sunshine, says me.

Few of us realise that South Africa long ago ceased to be a leading gold mining country. Most of what was up for grabs has already been grabbed, yanked and pulled from the ground.

From a country that dug shiny bits from the earth and sold apples on the side, we're today a diversified manufacturing and services-based economy. In simple terms, we make stuff and we sell it to the world.

So it's better the rand is where it's at because unyielding currencies don't build export-led economies. Yes, strong currencies make importing capital equipment cheaper but those are primarily once-off purchases. How many big yellow vehicles do you need? All strong currencies do is make overseas holiday booze cheaper while encouraging citizens to order more rubbish online they don't need.

What's the Japanese yen to the US dollar? About 140! Exactly. As Australia's now non-existent car industry discovered, no-one's interested in what you have to sell when your currency's too big for its boots.

It's kiff that South Africa is moving in the right direction buoyed by its people's long-time recognition of education as the way to achieve a better life. Moving things along faster is the growing pervasiveness of technology as evidenced by the regular launching of new coding, gaming and mobile technology initiatives of which Braamfontein's Tshimologong digital innovation precinct, the GirlCode initiative to empower 10m SA women with tech skills by 2030, Geekulcha's work to get youngsters digitally excited and the country's growing tally of Science Centres are just a few examples to highlight SA's priorities.

Our appreciation of education, the growing adoption of technology and our embracing of hustle culture is seeing millions connect the dots from graft to glory. I'm so excited about the next ten years. South Africa's Linkedin profile is really going to look kiff.

24

Neighbourhood Watches Move From Boots to Bytes

Two early encounters with the neighbourhood watch system stand out for me.

The first was around 1992 (my matric year) and involved nothing more than noticing a yellow sign on a lamppost with a menacing black-clad figure in what looked like a fedora hat prominently displayed. I could be forgiven for thinking it was a fedora, by the way, because close by was a sign prohibiting 'horse-drawn traffic'.

Somewhere on the yellow sign it was announced that the neighbourhood watch was in town. I remember thinking, 'what for?', such was the bubble for the fortunate few in '92! I could also never figure out this kak marketing because it seemed like the spooky figure on the yellow sign was being unwittingly elevated to some sort of anti-hero status. Every time I walked past that sign, I thought: "This makes no sense. People will want to be the cool guy in the cape with the fedora."

Of course, many people did want to be that guy and the rest is history. Let's fast-forward past some 30 years of electric fence installations and tens of millions of alarm activations to a more recent South Africa where I had my second memorable encounter with a neighbourhood watch.

We had moved to a very safe area (so safe that my wife forgot her laptop on the car roof in the morning and it was still there at the end of the day – making me wonder what she did the whole day) and, one morning, I was annoyed to be stuck behind a car with neighbourhood watch magnetic decals on it going about 30 km/h, clearly on some sort of community patrol.

At the time, I remember thinking - as in 1992 - 'what for?'. I mean, the area was clearly safe and these two tannies were obviously retired with nothing better to do than look through people's windows and cross-examine the homeless as they snailed around at 30 km/h.

It was kak that I was so wrong. Before we get into the general kiffness of neighbourhood watches in South Africa, and the unexpected mind, body and soul benefits this loose collective brings to communities and individuals alike, I want to take a moment to deal with the usual boring sentiment that says neighbourhood watches are not kiff because their mere existence signals policing failures. How typical of those who whine, how negative of those who provide no solutions, how uninformed of those who should know better, and how disappointing for those who try.

The fedora-wearing baddie of my school-going years above was, of course, an import. This image has been reproduced on countless neighbourhood watch signs erected in thousands of communities worldwide. To suggest the emergence of neighbourhood watches points to the general and worldwide collapse of global policing is just silly.

Neighbourhood watches in South Africa and elsewhere don't fill a policing vacuum. They make policing more effective. Where policing vacuums do exist, there's neighbourhood lynching, not neighbourhood watching!

The European Crime Prevention Network (ECPN) in 'Effects of Neighbourhood Watch in Reducing Crime' found that the introduction of a neighbourhood watch in an area was 'followed by a reduction in crime of between 16 and 26 percent'. The review notes that exactly why neighbourhood watches are effective is not known.

What is clear, however, is that the neighbourhood watch is not a South African invention. It does not, therefore, point to some uniquely South African-style collapse of local policing. Rather, our adoption of this globally-growing community safety intervention is South Africa taking the best the world has to offer and making it more effective where we live.

Community safety in South Africa is getting better in those communities that have implemented neighbourhood watches - in partnership with the SAPS, private security and with CPFs tying it all together.

From solely boots on the ground, the majority of South African neighbourhood watches have gone state-of-the-art. The rollout of fibre optic cable from the suburbs to the townships has enabled the introduction of street corner cameras and CCTV monitoring schedules by neighbourhood watches countrywide.

Now, those two low-speed tannies can use high-speed broadband to switch from vehicle-based car patrolling to smartphone-based camera monitoring. Not everyone is cut out for street patrolling, so technology is leading to more community members getting involved in their own safety.

Generally, any suspicious incidents seen by community members on neighbourhood watch-managed cameras are immediately flagged via Whatsapp to private security who will investigate and call for police assistance in the event of something serious.

From that imported yellow neighbourhood watch warning sign of dubious value from decades ago, neighbourhood watches in South Africa have emerged as effective community assets delivering more benefits to communities than simply protection from criminals.

We saw this during Covid-19 and during the Day Zero water scarcity emergency of several years ago. How fortunate for many vulnerable community members around South Africa that their local neighbourhood watches knew who and where they were.

Recent fire emergencies in Greece, California, Canada and Australia could have been mitigated by the existence of highly-localised, South African-style neighbourhood watches that are, actually, a commendable type of civil defence partnership built on deep community participation.

The modern neighbourhood watch, less about boots and more about bytes, is also morphing into something that's less about skiet and more about social. South Africa's NWs are helping the country's communities rediscover the joy of neighbourliness. Criminals, it seems, have failed, while we have won back Mr Wilson over the fence.

25

The Kiffness of a Kinder South Africa

From the ethereal 'ubuntu' that needs no explanation to the formalised kindness of Mandela Day, South Africa has emerged as a country of conscience where making a difference is a way of life.

For most of the fortunate throughout South Africa's recent history, charity amounted to little more than a handout begrudgingly given in a plastic packet or dished out in enamelware. A few times a year, you'd buy a sticker for something. Then The Big Issue made its appearance at the traffic lights and on your dashboard.

Make no mistake, South Africa is a place where inimitable acts of kindness have always existed. Many of us have first-hand knowledge of disadvantaged children being adopted by those better off. Countless and incredible non-profit organisations have been founded. We all grew up knowing those handful of volunteers in our communities who did the lion's share of the good work.

However, this all existed on the fringes of a brutalised society. I remember South Africa being a little laid-back and a lot aggressive. Maybe it was those micro-shorts, or the brandy and coke, or PW and his angry Peter Pointer. Was it the landmines, riots and rubber bullets and a whole lot of other crazy kak that everyone over 45 who complains about potholes has forgotten?

Fortunately, something started changing when Madiba and FW started appearing in public together and the seeds of reconciliation and kindness were planted. The 'New South Africa' and a different way of interacting with each other were introduced. I can still remember one of the print adverts about the 'New South Africa'. It seems so long ago but the 'ubuntuness' of the campaign is very familiar.

The country's new Constitution then made its appearance, building on our growing respect for each other by elevating the right to life as the cornerstone of the new South African state.

From 16 Days of Action, to the abovementioned Mandela Day, government and corporate South Africa are working together to spread the message of a much more humanistic, caring South Africa across multiple fronts. As I wrote elsewhere in this book, at least one foreign journalist believes South Africa has a lot in common with the liberal West.

Living here my entire adult life, sometimes I'm shocked by how right-wing much of the world has become while South Africa has steadily moved along a more chilled course. I love reading the mad stories in the New York Post, for example, but I can't get over how the paper can refer to the homeless as 'bums'. Imagine a South African journalist using that word! I'm not sure I would want to live in a place where 'bums' and 'beat downs' have worked their way into the local lingo.

I think I do want to live in a progressive place where the local sheriff can't throw you onto the street for a three-day late rental payment and where employers can't fire you without cause. Imagine being told thanks for the two decades but you're no longer a 'good fit' for the company. I'm not saying that doesn't happen in South Africa but, according to the law of the land, it shouldn't.

I see South Africa's new soft side in friends with their pet charitable projects, in neighbours and local businesses often fundraising for some or other good community cause, in companies that I work with always coming up with a public holiday plan of action that sees them doing something awesome in line with what's going down that day.

Young people in South Africa are fortunate that their first job often introduces them to people and projects they would not ordinarily be exposed to as paid-up members of the middling sort. South Africa uniquely positions us to do good.

South Africa is indeed becoming a fairer society with a great number of us fulfilled in the act of giving or otherwise doing good things. From wanting government to rescue every little situation, a lot more of us now link our own action, or inaction, to South Africa's future fortunes. This really is the place to live if you're more than the sum total of your Smeg appliances.

26

Far From Up and Away, We Want to Stay

Emigration is kak until you take your head out of the sand and realise every nation loses some of its educated and ambitious to the next biggest economy or most promising opportunity of the moment.

New Zealanders go to Australia, Australians go to the UK, the Brits and Canadians go to America and the Americans stay put building walls against everyone else.

The fact that South Africa produces some skills for export has been happening for decades. South Africa and emigration are not newlyweds. Since at least the 1960s, many South African doctors, for example, qualified at Wits and UCT and immediately left the country to avoid national service. Today they'll tell you from Toronto and Sydney they had a problem with the political system. I wonder how many did anything to dent apartheid after their departure?

So many professions lost qualified South Africans over many decades. Yet, without them, the country still managed to triple the gross value of all the goods and services it produces over the past thirty years and successfully transitioned from a minerals to a manufacturing economy. These are indisputable facts, as are the country's declining fertility rate, increasing life expectancy and declining debt-to-GDP ratio.

Wanting to spread one's wings or simply dodge the draft is nothing new and certainly not unique to South Africans. What's encouraging to me, however, in the local instance - and this signals progress in my mind - is that people expressing a desire to emigrate today no longer routinely bash the country.

In former times, crime was always trotted out as the number one reason to leave South Africa. It trumped all else and everyone would get very loud and emotional about 'the crime'. Rightfully so? No, not if you never lifted your arse to join or donate a few bob to your neighbourhood watch. Much easier to haul it halfway across the world than haul it up and down the street once in a while.

So insults about South Africa and her people, together with nasty predictions about her future, would usually accompany the potential émigré's self-righteous pontificating about 'getting out' (apparently, it's the last days of Batista's Havana here every day).

Economic reasons now seem to have topped crime as the would-be emigrant's reason for leaving. And people don't seem quite so angry anymore. To me, this is further evidence of the normalisation of all things South African. Leaving one's home to search for work is normal in every corner of the globe. People leaving South Africa, a lot less angry, and citing jobs and careers is a lot better than citing rape and murder on the way out. It means crime is still there, but it has stabilised as less of an existential threat, enabling the routine bread and butter issues of a normal society to emerge as the concerns of the day. Not great, but progress in a sense.

Fortunately, South Africa has so much to offer compared to the mediocre quality of life in many other countries that it remains a destination for the ambitious, educated and adventurous from across the globe. So yes, there are indeed people 'coming in'. Up to 10m tourists visit South Africa annually. Many fall in love with what's so obvious to them and forgotten by many of us so they choose to stay. The southern tip of Africa remains a people magnet as foreign accents suggest daily.

I remember a time when the media variously told us that 'a million' South Africans either live in the UK or had left the country. Actually, the 2021 UK census recorded 211 447 South African-born people residing in England. Unless you think there are 800 000-odd South Africans holed up in Scotland, that 'one million South Africans in the UK' figure was always rubbish. Incidentally, 200k is not very many if you consider this is all South African-born people, alive now. If you were born in SA in 1950 and went to the UK permanently in 1951, you're in the 200k. So not very many at all, relatively speaking.

Interestingly, after finishing this chapter, the 'one million' figure popped up again in another news wire hatchet job on South Africa and its 'struggles', this time reinventing itself as 900 000 South Africans who have left the country in the last 20 years. The stat was simply thrown out into the news ether, totally unreferenced and unsubstantiated.

However, if we for a moment accept that 900 000 South Africans out of 60m have left the country over the past 20 years; that's 45 000 a year, it doesn't account for returning South Africans nor new arrivals (it's not a net figure), and is significantly less than the 92 000 British citizens, for example, who leave the UK each year. Considering that South Africa has been an open democracy with a GDP that's tripled over the past 30 years, it's perfectly predictable - and indeed a positive thing - that our citizens of all races have the education and the increasing means to spread their rainbow-feathered wings across the world. It would be very strange, and even more worrying, if the citizens of an upper middle income country of 60m people did not travel.

Estimates of emigration are tricky because a number of South Africans do return (often accompanied by a soon-to-be South African), some after two months, some after two years (my close relatives) and some after 20 years (my neighbour). Some go the whole hog and emigrate financially, as SARS calls it, but others maintain business and property links for many years after leaving and return now and again. So how does one factor in all of this?

My own estimate after years of following the emigration issue is that significantly less than 20 000 South Africans of all races cut the cord each year. As we see above, when it comes to the Brits, not tens of thousands, but hundreds of thousands leave their damp island annually. This year, the Daily Mail says a 'record number' of Britons are planning to emigrate. It would be dangerous territory to get into the reasons, save to say that things have changed.

Whatever the rationale, the latest estimates on migration from the UK's Office for National Statistics (ONS) reveal:

"In the year ending December 2022 approximately 557,000 people emigrated from the United Kingdom, 92,000 of which were British citizens, 202,000 were EU citizens, and a further 263,000 were non-EU citizens." So even if one looks only at the 92k British citizen statistic above, that's a helluva lot of people leaving a country of a similar size to South Africa. So it seems a British passport is good for sunburns in Spain and permanently getting out of Britain.

When it comes to Australia, here's a headline from the Guardian last year: "Mass exodus: Australia faces loss of 600,000 people". The year before, Australia's own statistics bureau wrote in a press release: "More people emigrated from, than immigrated into, Australia in 2020-21". I'm not engaged in anything else here other than reminding you that people move and they don't only move from South Africa. In fact, an Australian government website says: 'At any time, there are around one million Australians living and working overseas.' Gosh, also 'a million'. Methinks the media is mixing us up again, like when they said Rodriguez was huge in Australia.

Funny how a million Aussies overseas are 'living and working' but a million South Africans overseas have 'left the country'. It's the same reason no-one has ever heard of an ex-American, ex-Scot or ex-anything else, but apparently we're all ex-South Africans the moment we're overseas for longer than a package holiday.

Aside from the oft-repeated, never backed-up 'one million' nasty above, we're also told 'thousands' of South Africans are emigrating annually. Our rainbow feathers must mean we can fly because we're also 'flocking' overseas (the grand total of 1 300-odd South Africans on the Isle of Man apparently amounts to a flock – what a scream). Doesn't this 'thousands' descriptor in headlines, actually, point to the general kiffness of the country? By attempting to beat the negative drum and specifically referring to 'thousands' of people emigrating, click-driven media platforms are, in fact, reinforcing the reverse because 'thousands' doesn't sound like a very serious issue to me. Does it to you? 'Thousands' of émigrés in a 60m-person economy with a growing middle class – not a dwindling one – sounds quite kiff. And good for them, send your money back and buy that beach house at R24 to the pound. Let your colleagues retire in the rain.

If it were totally kak here, would we not be seeing 'tens of thousands' or indeed, 'hundreds of thousands' of South Africans leaving? This is an upper middle income country (I'm sorry I keep beating that drum but this basic, unappreciated fact needs to get out there – we are far from poverty struck) – and millions have the means to leave. The average South African salary is hovering around R30 000 per month – more than enough for a visa and a ticket.

If you really think the only globally-mobile amongst us are the ones with a British passport, you must have fish and chips in your head. Where there's a will, there's a way. I mean, I only have to think of some of the people I know who have gone to Australia and New Zealand – most are not exactly the crème de la crème by any stretch of the imagination.

Think about it, in the face of all our overblown but still weighty issues, the absolute overwhelming majority of South Africans, across all racial groups and incomes, are choosing to remain in their country and have no desire to leave permanently. Like the East Germans, do people not vote with their feet? What people say they want to do when they're around the braai and what they actually end up doing are usually two very different things. A lot of us bleat at the BBQ, look around us on the way home, and decide what we have here is too good to give up for what they have there.

Many of us will say it's mostly white South Africans leaving the country and that's somehow worse than the rest of us leaving. Um, not any more. The economy, tax base and ranks of professionals running the country are no longer so dependent on the former ruling class. Sorry for your ego. In any event, Stats SA says in the five years from 2021 to 2026: "outward migration for the white population group... will be about 43 516." That's about 8 700 white South Africans leaving annually out of a population of about 4.5m to 4.6m. Peanuts, boet.

Ireland has a population of about 5.0m people. MigrantProject.ie says 22 800 Irish people emigrated in the year to April 2021. Well, well. But wait, there's more. Denmark also has a 5m-odd population of comparable size to South Africa's white population. Statista says, in 2022, a total of 69 927 people emigrated from Denmark. Is that because the First World is so awesome?

Several thousand whites leaving South Africa annually is so tiny as to be irrelevant. In fact, the only negative here seems to be that we're a lazy bunch. Good luck getting this lot off their bums and into the sea, Mr Malema.

27

SAS South Africa: Slowly Going Somewhere Kiff

There was a time when we thought that South Africa was so fragile that any number of single negative events could sink it.

Everything from Nelson Mandela's refusal to suspend the armed struggle, to the assassination of Chris Hani with invasions of Angola, high interest rates, the always-crashing rand, national shutdowns, Day Zero and Covid-19 in between have been viewed at some point as total calamities for the country. It's kiff now that South Africans are starting to develop a sense of 'relax, we've been here before'.

The bad weather events keep rolling in - always looking like they're going to wreck the ship - but to the surprise and consternation of all who continue to wrongly predict her imminent destruction, SAS South Africa keeps ploughing on as the waves break over her.

The more sage and calmer amongst us have developed a sense of perspective that's possibly lacking amongst younger South Africans, newer arrivals or those who were overseas or too busy jolling in the 80s and 90s to read the news. The message from the former to the latter must be: Stop going off the deep end. It's time to put an end to 125-odd years of incorrect, SA-focused negativity.

I love the ship analogy because it leaves room for amusing thoughts of many captains struggling at the wheel while taxis race around the promenade deck and one hell of a party continues in total darkness below.

Ah yes, SAS South Africa. It's pirate-style fun aboard, rolls side-to-side but inexplicably for the smart Economists, never actually capsizes and keeps slowly moving forward. She defies all logic. Moreover, a third of the passengers can't find anything useful to do, the deck is full of holes and there's no electrical power to the engines. Yet, everyone's in a surprisingly good mood, cracks jokes at every opportunity and wants to talk as the water occasionally rushes in.

There's a serious message amongst this silliness and it's that the events that keep hitting us do not result in our country's destruction because they are small beer. Our problems are challenges and that's all they are.

In fact, when a country is faced with an existential threat, it's usually clear to all and sundry what this single event actually is. In history, it's been the Nazis, hyperinflation and coups. When the media today writes about the supposed failed state-style issues facing South Africa, they can't even name one convincing mega-issue. All that can be done is conflate a collection of vague issues in an effort to sound like it's all going to pot. These attempts are unconvincing and they signal a media that's gone from writing fact to opinion-based 'news'.

One recent emigration-themed article about South Africa by an international newswire service I won't name, when presenting reasons for South Africans leaving, could think of no actual specifics, only mentioning these vague beauties: 'the political landscape', 'policy paralysis', 'the country's future', 'continual power cuts' (I'll give you that one, although the use of the word 'continual' is debatable), 'security concerns' (the vaguest of all) and 'economic downswing' (factually incorrect – we've had just one recent quarter of negative GDP growth). All of those, bar one, are unconvincing for their lack of expected news-related specificity.

Elsewhere, there is major kak going down on planet earth and, for many countries, it's deeply unsolvable. You can also easily name the threats. It's not 'policy paralysis' in Ukraine – it's the Russians. It's not 'the country's future' in the UK – it's 660 plus people a day arriving in rubber boats (Sky News) and it's 120 knife crime incidents every day in England and Wales (Evening Standard).

Yes, major unsolvable, very specific scary kak worldwide. Unfortunately, you can't move Western Europe away from war. The US can't shrink back into itself for a peaceful future. The UK will never warm up enough. The land of the long white cloud will stay beautiful – and wet. Liberal democracy is not the way of China nor what it wants in its backyard. You can't move a poorly-positioned country into some sort of relevance. Snow is too much snow. Landlocked is landlocked. Those countries that catch fire every year are only going to light up more often. A country without much water is set to become a country with no water. Some are set to sink into the water. The desert can't ever be greened enough. Salt water will stay salty. Anomaly states that are at odds with the people and landscape surrounding them are unsustainable.

When you look at the bigger picture in this way, you realise that we've landed with our bums in the butter because all our problems are made by ourselves! What's the implication? It's obvious – we can solve them ourselves, like we did with apartheid. There is no deep-seated crazy racial or religious hatred here. Remarkably, we get on well. Our only potential for natural disasters lies in the fact that sometimes it's too wet in KZN and too dry in the Karoo.

If we look at current events in Ukraine, Israel, Lebanon, Northern Ireland, Taiwan, and of course the madness always going down in the US, to name just a few of the usual suspects (forgive the pun, America), one realises that these forever hotspots have intractable problems.

Our own issues, conversely, are so small. I'm not discounting, for example, gender-based violence and grinding poverty, but those who keep predicting SAS South Africa's imminent grounding and dashing to pieces, are more prone to raising the embarrassingly-tiny issues of potholes, burst water pipes, lippy licensing officials, speeding taxis, classrooms with 33 kids, overweight traffic cops and four-hour waits at government hospitals.

As I said, tiny, solvable issues. What's more, as we see in communities countrywide, South Africans do not sit idly by. We are used to fixing things and fix it all, we will.

www.ingramcontent.com/pod-product-compliance
Lightning Source LLC
Chambersburg PA
CBHW060738280326
41933CB00032B/2891

* 9 7 8 0 7 9 6 1 1 4 1 9 8 *